Nigeria–
United States Relations

Perspectives on
Political Change in Africa

Smart Uhakheme

UNIVERSITY PRESS OF AMERICA, ® INC.
Lanham • Boulder • New York • Toronto • Plymouth, UK

Copyright © 2008 by
University Press of America,® Inc.
4501 Forbes Boulevard
Suite 200
Lanham, Maryland 20706
UPA Acquisitions Department (301) 459-3366

Estover Road
Plymouth PL6 7PY
United Kingdom

Library of Congress Control Number: 2007936548
ISBN-13: 978-0-7618-3919-4 (paperback : alk. paper)
ISBN-10: 0-7618-3919-4 (paperback : alk. paper)

This book is dedicated to my parents Mesharun and Olobi for their love, inspiration and support.

Contents

List of Tables

Preface

This study centers on Nigeria-United States relations, focusing on both countries' perspectives on political change in Africa in the waning years of decolonization. It is premised on the assumption that international politics is generally a mix of conflictual and cooperative relationships. It is in this context that the study examines Nigeria-United States perspectives, and the positions taken by both countries on the issue of political change in Africa, using Angola, Zimbabwe, Namibia and South Africa as case studies.

The study shows that, at the level of diplomatic rhetoric, there seemed to be a shared perspective on political change between Nigeria and the United States. However, underneath this shared perspective lie a host of disagreements and differences. Of critical significance were the differences in the interpretation of political change and the motivations behind both countries' policy in Southern Africa.

Nigeria favored radical change, while the United States favored gradual change. Furthermore, it was clear that Nigeria was motivated by its commitment to the cause of African emancipation, while the United States was largely motivated by its varied economic and strategic interests in the region. These differences however, did not make cooperation between both countries in other areas impossible. United States supported pro-democracy movement during Nigeria's long struggle with military dictatorship, and Nigeria returned the favor by giving strong support for United States counter terrorism efforts; cooperated with the U.S. in its campaign against international drug trafficking and financial crimes, and as Assistant Secretary of State for Africa, Jendayi Frazer puts it, Nigeria remains a strategic country to the United States security, trade and oil needs. And as of March 2007 Nigeria accounts for 12 per cent of United States oil imports, making Nigeria the third largest oil supplier to the United States, surpassing Venezuela and Saudi Arabia.

On the whole, Nigeria-United States relations during the period under study were marked by disagreements and cooperation. Relations between the two countries were decidedly cool at times, cordial at other times and uneasy for many years.

Acknowledgments

The impetus to write this book evolved while I was a graduate student at Atlanta University (now Clark Atlanta University) where I received considerable assistance and encouragement from many people, some of whom deserve particular mention. Among these are: Drs. Robert Holmes, Shelby Lewis, Ken Eke, Earl Picard, Hashim Gibrill and George Kugblenu.

I also want to thank my colleagues and friends at Bethune-Cookman University, especially Dr. John Ukawuilulu, Department of Gerontology, and my Dean Dr. Russell Mootry Jr. for their useful comments and encouragement to finish this book. I am grateful for the assistance I received from the library personnel at Atlanta University, Georgia State University, Bethune-Cookman University, and the Nigerian Institute of International Affairs. A special thanks to Valerie Kendrick for helping me chase down footnotes and typing the manuscript.

Above all, I owe a huge debt of gratitude to my family for their love and encouragement, especially my son Eghe, for assisting me in mastering the latest in computer technology and my wife 'Kpabomo for her unwavering love and personal sacrifices.

Chapter One

Introduction

Immediately after Nigeria's independence in 1960, Africa became the centre point of its foreign policy. The promotion of African unity and the achievement of total political, economic, social and cultural liberation of Africa were two of its stated foreign policy objectives.

Over the years, Nigeria has spent a lot of political and economic capital in pursuit of these objectives. In attempting to achieve these objectives, Nigeria realized that there were other important actors in the international environment to contend with. One such actor was the United States, whose stated global policy, at that time included: (1) wider cooperation with key allies and close cooperation with such regional influential nations as Nigeria, Saudi Arabia and Brazil; (2) strengthening its presence in all regions of the world; and (3) enhancing its cooperative effort with "moderate states of Africa in the cause of African emancipation.[1]

Nigeria-United States relations have not always been ambiguous. In the period covered by this study, a discernible pattern was apparent. Relations between both countries had their high and low points since Nigerian independence in 1960. The United States alleged support for Biafra during the Nigerian civil war resulted in strained relations in 1967–70. Also there were open differences over the United States involvement in Angola in 1975, culminating in the unwillingness of Nigeria to receive the then Secretary of State Henry A. Kissinger. However, relations between both countries improved immensely during the Carter administration largely due to the skillful diplomacy of Andrew Young, then United States Ambassador to the United Nations. There were cordial exchanges and visits between 1977 and 1980, first Jimmy Carter and then Vice President Walter Mondale visited Nigeria. And, in October 1980 it was President Shehu Shagari's turn to reciprocate with a visit to the United States. There were those who thought that despite these visits nothing of substance was actually accomplished.

AN EXPLORATORY STUDY IN
CONFLICT AND COOPERATION

Every nation state in the contemporary state system has its own national interests that differ from the interests of other nations. These differences may sometimes lead to clashes. Occasional clashes between nation states notwithstanding, they will engage in cooperative efforts in other areas. As Ivo D. Duchacek puts it, nation states "may often have profound disagreements on trade and tariff policies while their political and military cooperation flourishes.[2]

Furthermore, it needs to be said that virtually all relationships contain some elements of conflict. Even in the most cooperative relationship between nation states, some areas of disagreement are bound to occur. According to Duchacek, "no two nations can be expected to have all their interests in harmony with one another all the time," nor do they "have all their interests in conflict all the time." Even arch enemies, Duchacek added, are often able to engage in cooperative relationship in one sector "while uncompromising enmity and total distrust prevail in a different sector of their relations."[3]

The implication here is that international politics is a mix of conflictual and cooperative relationships. They are not mutually exclusive. That is, nation states can be engaged in both relationships at the same time. It is in this context that this study will analyze Nigeria-United States relations with respect to their perspectives on political change in Africa, using Angola, Zimbabwe, Namibia, and South Africa as case studies.

Areas of Disagreements

At least five areas of conflict between Nigeria and the United States can be identified: (1) the United States' refusal to sell arms to Nigeria during the Biafran conflict and the alleged United States support for Biafra, (2) United States involvement in Angola in 1975, (3) whether or not Nigeria would use its oil as an instrument of its foreign policy toward the United States, (4) the rate at which Nigeria should be producing its oil and the price at which it should be sold to the United States, and (5) whether Nigeria should be considered a rich country. These will be elaborated upon elsewhere in the book.

COOPERATION

These areas of conflict did not make cooperation between both countries in other areas impossible. Both countries were involved in cooperative efforts to find a solution to the problem of colonialism in Southern Africa. Lately these areas of cooperation have been expanded upon to include: containing regional conflicts, peacekeeping operations, fighting crime and corruption, and international terrorism.

Did the United States need Nigeria's understanding? Was it important to the United States that Nigeria remained a friendly nation? Was Nigeria's support for United States diplomatic initiatives in Africa crucial to the success of those initiatives? Conversely, was Nigeria's opposition an important factor in the failure of those initiatives? Did United States diplomatic initiatives, when successful, benefit both countries?

A major theme in the history of independence struggles in Africa was total political, economic, social and cultural liberation of Africa. Political change, recognized then and now as a fundamental right to be sought; its achievement came with a heavy toll, and Africans came out of the struggle bruised and battered.

History of Approaches to Independence

By the early 1960s the rise of numerous independent African states helped legitimize two approaches to political independence; negotiated settlement and revolution. The form of government that was put in place after political independence was to a large extent, determined by which approach was taken. Apart from the Congo crisis where the Kennedy administration played a major role in the installation of Mobutu as a brutal dictator and the demise of Lumumba, United States interest was not reawakened until 1975 when Portuguese domination was suddenly dismantled. Chester A. Crocker explained: "Washington could no longer simply enjoy its varied interests in Africa: it would have to work actively to preempt Soviet-backed revolutionary change and deter further communist adventurism.[4]

By 1960, the first wave of political independence swept through the African continent, and observers were certain that political change in Africa was inevitable. There was evidence to show that political change per se was not necessarily inimical to United States interests. As the movement for political independence was gathering momentum, United States policy makers came to the realization that the United States would no longer act as the policeman of Africa, preventing change. Instead they realized that what was needed was the management of change to fit in with United States aspirations and interests. A study by the Center for Strategic and International Studies concluded that what matters was not the fact of change but how change occurs, whose interests and influence it reflects, and the extent of violent or coercive solutions.[5]

How important to Nigeria was the issue of political change in Africa? How sensitive was United States foreign policy to this issue? How did both countries manage their differences and find a common ground on how best to achieve political change in Africa?

POLITICAL CHANGE

Political scientists are not agreed on the precise meaning of political change. However, there seems to be a consensus that it involves the reordering of a given political system to permit all adult members of the population an effective participation in the political process.

Pan-Africanists hold the view that political change in Africa means "radical redistribution of power and wealth."[6] Martin Kilson defines political change as "the alteration in the ideas, values, procedures, and institutions concerned with the role of authority, power, influences, and government."[7] Radical Pan-Africanists take the definition a little further by asserting that the outcome of such a restructuring of the political system should be a socialist order.[8]

All of these definitions are useful, but for the purpose of this study, a suitable definition relates to the seizure of power that leads to a major restructuring of government and society, as distinguished from the mere replacement of the former elite by a new one or coup d' etat involving no more than a change of ruling personnel. Put simply, political change means the wresting of state power from colonial and neo-colonial governments, occupation forces, settler regimes, minority regimes, and the fundamental restructuring of the political system. The ultimate goal is to maximize a state's political, economic, social and cultural liberation. This can be brought about by one or a combination of two approaches: (a.) armed struggle, and (b) negotiated settlement. The adoption of one approach does not necessarily preclude the other—in other words, they are not mutually exclusive. Nigeria publicly embraces both approaches, while the United States publicly adopts (b), but covertly encourages (a) in a sometimes futile attempt to prevent change that would lead to a fundamental restructuring of government and society. At the level of diplomatic rhetoric, both countries seemed to hold similar views on political change, but does political change mean the same thing to both nations?

FUNDAMENTAL DIFFERENCES IN INTERPRETATION

Nigeria

During the period covered by this study, particularly beginning with the Muhammed administration, Nigeria adopted a radical and militant approach to issues relating to the liberation of Southern Africa. To Nigeria, political change had come to mean the wresting of state power from a colonial regime and the fundamental restructuring of the political system. Nigeria believed that this could be attained by: (a) peaceful means where feasible, and (b) armed struggle when necessary. Furthermore, Nigeria was strongly in favor of radical change and total liberation, as opposed to the mere changing of the ruling personnel. An indication of Nigeria's commitment to radical change could be seen from her extensive support for liberation movements in Africa.

United States

Historically, the United States' position could be summed up as follows: (a) rhetorical condemnation of colonialism, and (b) at the same time, expressing its strong opposition to armed struggle. Chester Crocker reiterated this position when he said that the United States cannot endorse colonialism or oppression, nor those who are "dedicated to seizing or holding power through violence." To the United States, political change meant no more than a mere change of ruling personnel, with little or no change in the structure of the political system and society. It has a history of supporting evolutionary change, as opposed to radical change. It sought negotiation, but opposed armed struggle that would lead to radical change. It needs to be said that although the United States was opposed to armed struggle as an official policy, it was also involved in covert operations in many trouble spots around the world.

In sum, there were differences in both countries' interpretations of political change in important respects. While Nigeria favored fundamental change, the United States did not. Instead, the United States favored evolutionary change. Furthermore, Nigeria favored both peaceful means and armed struggle to bring about change, but the United States favored peaceful change, and only opposed armed struggle as an official policy, but favored covert operations. There was evidence to suggest that the United States: (a) was only opposed to armed struggle that would lead to fundamental restructuring of government and society, and (b). actively supported armed struggle in Cuba (Bay of Pigs), Vietnam, Angola, Nicaragua and Grenada to either maintain a status quo or overthrow a government it considered unfriendly.

The question that needs to be asked is why was the United States, a country born of revolution, opposed to radical change? Part of the answer can be gleaned from the discussion of United States interests and motivations elsewhere in this book.

At least two time periods are discernible in the literature on Nigeria-United States relations. There are those who contend that prior to 1975, and for the most part of the Nixon/Ford administration, relations between both countries were at an all time low. Others state that beginning with the Carter administration, relations between both countries significantly improved.

Prior to 1975 Nigeria was referred to as a "sleeping giant" because of its inactive, low profile and sometimes timid foreign policy posture. Critics say Nigeria's low profile and timid foreign policy posture was a calculated attempt by successive governments from 1960 to 1975 to: "stave off direct conflict with any of the major powers except on critical issues such as the preservation of the sovereignty, territorial integrity and independence of Nigeria."[9]

Nigeria's low profile foreign policy posture coincided with another important fact in the international system—the East-West power struggle. Cold War concerns, the war in Vietnam and Russian activities in Cuba were of paramount importance to Washington; therefore, the formulation of a credible United States Nigerian policy was a low priority issue for United States policymakers. Joseph Wayas, Senate President in the First Republic noted that "of all the areas of the world, only Antarctica is less important to the United States,"[10] than Nigeria or Africa. President Lyndon B. Johnson's presumed indifference or ignorance was depicted by his quoted remarks to British Prime Minister Harold Wilson in 1964: "I keep confusing Nigeria and Algeria because both end in 'geria.' In the first decade and a half after Nigeria's independence, U.S. policy toward Nigeria was either nonexistent or one of benign neglect.

In the last days of the Ford Administration, Secretary of State Henry A. Kissinger started to move away from the policy of benign neglect. In an attempt to improve relations between both countries, a more active diplomacy with Nigeria was initiated as evidenced by a scheduled official visit to Nigeria by Kissinger. Although the visit was later cancelled, [11]diplomatic observers were convinced that a change in Nigeria-United States relations was imminent. However, Kissinger's move away from the policy of benign neglect had not gone unnoticed in Nigeria. This shift was attributed to "the intervention of Cuban troops in Angola and the subsequent routing of Western-backed forces in the former Portuguese colony.[12]

When Murtala Muhammad came to power in 1975 in a coup d'etat in which Yakubu Gowon was overthrown, the time had come for the "sleeping giant" to wake up. Subsequent foreign policy decisions taken by the Muhammad administration led Africanists to characterize Nigeria's foreign policy as a "dynamic" one. Observers said that such change in Nigeria's foreign policy approach was long overdue. Nigeria, "seems to have finally arrived at the role and status which Nigerians have been clamoring for since 1960."[13] This arrival of Nigeria was precipitated by the enormous resources generated by the oil boom, resources which were then being ploughed into industrial and infrastructural bases. Jean Herskovits recognized this potential power, and warned that if Nigeria translates its potential into actual power, the United States would have to "rethink its policies and actions in Africa."[14]

The dynamic foreign policy of the Muhammad administration facilitated by the new wealth coincided with the ascendancy of Jimmy Carter to the White House. When Carter announced that he planned to visit Nigeria, observers were quick to point out that a change in Nigeria-United States relations had emerged. President Jimmy Carter's visit to Nigeria was described as a symbol of "a new spirit" in Nigeria-United States relations. Chester A. Crocker and William H. Lewis thought that such a change was reflected by "top appointments and a highly energetic diplomacy." They explained:

> To offset past impressions of United States neglect, Washington's new approach was to define and take stock of the African view point on the continent's many problems. This meant extending the narrow base of past United States African diplomacy beyond traditional friends, and building ties with Nigeria . . . where previous relations had ranged from cool to icy.[15]

The Carter administration marked a significant turning point in Nigeria-United States relations. The Carter policy provided both countries with an opportunity for a fresh start and a realistic examination of issues affecting both countries. Donald B. Easum, the then United States Ambassador to Nigeria offered a summary of the change in Nigeria-United States relations:

> We take Nigerian views very seriously, and not just on African issues but on issues of global concern. We consult and discuss together such problems as the North-South economic relationship, or the Law of the Sea, or Zimbabwe and Namibia, or the question of political rights and equal opportunity within South Africa itself. Nigerian views on these issues are an increasingly important factor in the formulation of United States policies.[16]

The visits by General Obasanjo to the United States and President Carter to Nigeria, the strengthened economic links between both countries and Washington's firm stand on majority rule for Namibia and South Africa were some of the concrete examples of improved relations between both countries.

Critics said that in spite of what was done by both countries to improve relations, nothing of substances was actually accomplished. They saw more noise than substance to the Carter administration's vaunted claims of a new spirit in Nigeria-United States relations. Domestic constraints did not permit Carter to be as progressive as he would have liked to be in Africa.

Other limitations of the Carter administrations were the departure of some of the key members of the Africanists group in the administration, such as Andrew Young and later Secretary of State Cyrus Vance. The rival group, the Globalists, including National Security Adviser Zbigniew Brzezinski, seemed to have prevailed by the end of 1979 in influencing the administration's African policy.

If the new spirit in Nigeria-United States relations during the Carter administration, to a large extent, led to improved relations between both countries, what was the situation under the Reagan administration? Initially the Reagan administration made strong efforts to maintain good relations with Nigeria, partly for the same reasons the Carter administration did, recognizing the relationship as one of mutual dependence and that the areas of common interest between both countries needed to be emphasized. However, there was a growing uneasiness between both countries that became explicit and manifest during the first year of the Reagan administration. One of the first indications of the unease was the May 1981 visit of the South African Foreign Minister to the White House. This visit was describes as: officially signaling an end to almost three years of chilly relations between Washington and Pretoria . . . but it is certain to cause political problems for Reagan at home and abroad.[17]

The new African policy under Reagan was essentially coaxing rather than threatening South Africa into cooperation. This meant, as Leslie Gelb puts it:

> (1) Strengthening direct ties with South Africa through symbols like official visits and proposing terms for a Namibian settlement closer to Pretoria's wishes,
> (2) recognizing South Africa's problems with the White minority in South West Africa.[18]

The unease that characterized Nigeria-United States relations during the Reagan years slowed down the pace of decolonization, but did not prevent it.

THE PLAN OF THE BOOK

This book deals with Nigeria-U.S. relations during the first two decades of Nigerian Independence, 1960–1994. Chapter 1 is a general introduction. Chapter 2 is an overview of Nigeria-United States relations during the period covered by this research. Chapter 3 focuses on both countries' perspectives on political change. Chapter 4 is an analysis of the positions taken by both countries on the question of political change in Africa, using Angola, Zimbabwe, Namibia, and South Africa as case studies and Chapter 5 concludes the book with a reflection on relations between both countries, their perspectives on political change in Africa, and future prospects for Nigeria-United States relations.

NOTES

1. *National Security Council Strategy No. D18* (Washington: U.S. Government Printing Press, 1978), 15.

2. Ivo D. Duchacek, *Nations and Men* (Hindesdale, Ill.: Dryden Press 1975), 532.

3. Duchacek, Nations and Men, 532.

4. Chester A. Crocker et al., *The Implications of Soviet and Cuban Activities in Africa for U.S. Policy* (Washington, D.C.: U.S. Government Printing Office, 1979), 15.

5. Crocker et al., *The Implications*, 15.

6. Leonard Thompson and J. Butler, *Change in Contemporary South Africa* (Los Angeles: U.C.L.A. Press, 1975), XI.

7. Martin Kilson, *Political Change in a West African State* (Cambridge: Harvard Univ. Press, 1966), 281.

8. For detailed discussions of radical Pan-Africanists' view on political change, see Christopher Allen, *Radical Africana* (London: Merlin Press, 1974, and Claude Ake, *Revolutionary Pressures in Africa* (London: Zed Press, 1978).

9. Olajide Aluko, *Essays in Nigerian Foreign Policy* (Boston: Allen & Unwin, 1981), 240.

10. Olajide Aluko, *Essays in Nigerian* (Boston: Allen & Unwin, 1981), 240.

11. "Kissinger Can't Come Now," *Daily Sketch*, (Nigeria) 10 April 1976, 12.

12. "U.S. Afridan Policy Revisited," *Nigeria Standard*, 12 August 1976, 5. For further discussions of diplomacy, see "The Angola Fiasco," *Great Decisions* 1979, 58.

13. A Bolaji Akinyemi, *Nigerian Foreign Policy, in Nigerian Government and Politics*, ed. O. Oyediran (London: Macmillan, 1979), 167.

14. Jean Herskovits, "Nigeria: Africa's New Power," *Foreign Affairs* (January 1975): 314–33.

15. Chester A. Crocker and W.H. Lewis, "Missing Opportunities in Africa," *Foreign Policy* (Winter 1977–78): 142.

16. Donald B. Easum, *Interlink* No. 51 (1977): 10.

17. "Reagan Opens His Doors to South African Official," *Atlanta Constitution*, 16, May 1981, 6(A).

18. Leslie H. Gelb, "A New African Policy," *New York Times* 4 June 1981, 4 (Y).

Chapter Two

Overview of
Nigeria-United States Relations

This chapter provides: (a) brief background information on Nigeria's foreign policy in its early years as an independent nation, and (b) an overview of Nigeria-United States relations during the period under study, pointing out the low and the high points.

BACKGROUND

The hallmark of Nigeria's foreign policy in its early years after independence was "pragmatism, restraint and caution." This low-profile foreign policy posture has been interpreted to mean: (a) a decidedly pro-western bent, (b) avoidance of controversial issues, and (c) operating within the consensus of the Organization of African Unity (OAU), the precursor to African Union.[1] At independence in 1960 Nigeria's Prime Minister Sir Abubakar T. Balewa expressed his belief in "a flexible foreign policy and in a closer association" with the West. Under the first civilian government of Prime Minister Balewa (1960–1966) Nigeria was officially nonaligned, but was infact pro-West. At the United Nations, Nigeria supported western positions. Such a pro-western bent, reasoned Prime Minister Balewa, would "ensure that full attention is paid to the opinions" and views expressed by Nigeria on the important political issues of the time.[2] Nigeria's financial position at independence was very weak and she had to conduct herself in a manner acceptable to the west whose financial assistance Nigeria needed. And from 1960 to 1966 Nigeria received $273 million in foreign aid from the west.[3] This dependence on financial aid "imposed severe constraints on the options open to the Balewa regime in its foreign policy.

In the affairs of the continent, Nigeria did not exert herself. Essentially Nigeria adhered to the A.U. principles of:

(1) non-interference in the internal affairs of states, (2) respect for the sovereignty and territorial integrity of each state, (3) peaceful settlement of disputes by negotiation, mediation, conciliation or arbitration, and (4) absolute dedication to the total emancipation of the African territories which are still dependent.[4]

This meant that Nigeria had to wait to be part of an overall African consensus before taking any position on most issues affecting the continent. On southern Africa, however, Nigeria was more forceful. The crusade against colonialism and oppression was one of the cornerstones of Nigeria's foreign policy. On the 15th Anniversary of the Sharpeville Massacre, Nigeria's, then, Commissioner for External Affairs, Dr. O. Arikpo reiterated Nigeria's position:

It is the duty of not only the government but of all the people of Nigeria to support the diplomatic, economic and cultural isolation of South Africa until that country abandons racial discrimination; until that government treats the black man in South Africa as a full citizen of the country of his birth. . . .[5]

Nigeria backed these pronouncements up by taking the following actions: (a) prohibited South African passport holders from entry into Nigeria, (b) cut off trade with South Africa, (c) spearheaded the move that forcefully removed South Africa from the Commonwealth, and (d) played a key role in contesting the credentials of the South African delegations at many international forums. Balewa's government was overthrown in a coup that brought General Yakubu Gowon to power in 1966.

Yakubu Gowon's military regime that succeeded the Balewa administration at first followed the same low-profile course in foreign policy. However, with the beginning of the civil war in 1967, changes in Nigeria's foreign policy posture started to emerge. First, there was a change in emphasis. Nigeria placed more emphasis on acting independently of the west in foreign affairs. Second, there was a conscious attempt by Nigeria to curb its pro-western bent by encouraging relations with Russia (formerly Soviet Union). While the Balewa regime maintained economic and military ties almost exclusively with the West, the Gowon administration broke with tradition in August 1967 by entering into cultural, economic, and military aid agreements with Russia. On August 11, 1967 the first shipment of Russian MIG-17s and 122mm artillery batteries arrived in Nigeria with Russian military personnel. Trade with Russia also rose from 2.4 percent of Nigeria's total trade in 1966 to 4.6 percent in 1968.[6] Nigeria's attempt at strengthening its relations with Russia,

notwithstanding, its' cultural, economic and trade links remained securely
with the West.

Gowon was ousted in another coup in 1975. Observers contend that what
emerged at the end of the Gowon administration was a "transformation of
Nigeria's foreign policy into one of rigorous nonalignment."[7] This transformation was precipitated by the unwillingness of Britain and the United States
to supply arms to Nigeria during the civil war, and the alleged United States
support for Biafra.

In sum, Nigerian foreign policy under Prime Minister Balewa (1960–1966)
was officially nonaligned, with a strong commitment to the principles of AU
charter and a pro-western bent. The course of the civil war and western reactions and involvement precipitated a new stance in Nigeria's foreign policy
during Gowon administration (1966–1975). Gowon's rigorous nonalignment
policy meant curbing Nigeria's pro-western bent and reaching out to Russia.
Gowon's successor, Murtala Muhammad, changed all that.

Brigadier Olusegun Obasanjo became Chief of Staff, Supreme Headquarters and Colonel Garba became Commissioner for External Affairs. These
were critical appointments in that: (a) Muhammad and Obasanjo were vocal
members of the Nigerian foreign affairs elite, with critical views of Nigeria's
foreign policy under Gowon before assuming their positions, which meant, (b)
among other things, that the views of the professional staff and the Nigerian
academicians would no longer be disregarded as seemed to be the case under
Gowon. As expected, the new administration set up a high powered committee to review Nigeria's foreign policy.[8] Consequently, rather than maintain
continuity with his predecessors, Muhammad adopted a "radical and militant"
approach, not hesitating to engage in confrontation with any of the major powers, especially on issues relating to the liberation of Southern Africa.

Muhammad's approach, facilitated by the new oil wealth, did not fail to
arouse United States attention. Thus after about eight-year reign over United
States policy of benign neglect, Henry Kissinger, then the United States Secretary of State, attempted to visit Nigeria in 1976, thus, signaling a shift in
U.S. policy.

OVERVIEW

The years 1975 to 1976 can be characterized as the low point in Nigeria-
United States relations, while 1977 to 1980 represented the high point. Relations between Lagos and Washington were decidedly cool, if not icy during the
Nixon-Ford administrations. One of the manifestations of this was the unwillingness of Lagos to receive then Secretary of State, Henry A. Kissinger. It was

crystal clear that during this period the United States had no active Nigerian policy. According to Aluko, the main sources of disagreement between the two countries, among others, were: (1) the tough and uncompromising style of then Nixon-Ford administrations in dealing with African countries, American importation of strategic minerals from (Rhodesia) Zimbabwe until the repeal of the Byrd Amendment, and (3) the United States involvement in Angola in 1975, and the Ford letter to the Nigerian leader on the eve of the extraordinary summit meeting of the African Union in Addis Ababa in January 1977.[9]

Between 1977 and 1980 Nigeria-United States relations took a dramatic turn around from the open differences mentioned above to cordial exchanges which culminated in state visits by the leaders of both countries. Both visits were hailed in Lagos and Washington as a success. This heightened United States interest in Nigeria could be traced to three distinct causes, strategic, political, and economic.

Strategic

Russia-Cuban activities in Africa had cause United States policy-makers to recognize the need to cultivate the friendship of Nigeria. Such friendship with Nigeria and other key African countries, United States policy-makers envisaged, would be instrumental in the success of further United States diplomatic initiatives designed to curtail Russian-Cuban activities in Africa.

Political

The influence of about 25 million Americans of African ancestry who want to see justice done for the black majorities in Southern Africa denied effective political participation.

Economic

The value of United States investments in Nigeria had been considerable. The main sectors of United States investments were in the oil industry, liquefied gas, agriculture, construction, banking, and insurance and manufacturing industries. In 1980 United States trade and investments with Nigeria stood at $1.49 and $3.5 billion, respectively.[10]

Clearly the new understanding between Nigeria and the United States could be summed up in three principles:

(1) The key to success in black Africa is to establish the United States as a friend of African nationalism; (2) stronger pressures must be brought to bear against

white minority rule in Southern Africa; and (3) to accomplish the above, the United States must de-emphasize East-West confrontation in Africa.[11]

Some of the important reasons for the new understanding can be gleaned from a National Security Council Memorandum part of which sought to foster closer cooperation with Nigeria which was regarded as one of the influential states likely to sway the fate of the rest of Africa; and to enhance United States cooperative effort with the "moderate states of Africa in the cause of African emancipation."[12]

Undoubtedly there was a convergence of interests between the two countries. The "cause of African emancipation," for which the United States was willing to join forces with moderate African states to achieve, was also the main desire of Nigeria. The Carter administration made it known that its' ultimate goal in Southern Africa was the establishment of the principle of 'one man, one vote', which was what Nigeria also wanted. Because of this convergence of interests, Nigeria supported United States diplomatic initiatives in Africa.

In September 1977 Nigeria came out strongly in favor of the Anglo-American settlement proposals in Zimbabwe. According to Joseph Garba, then Nigeria's Commissioner for External Affairs, General Obasanjo's trip in September 1977 to the front line states was undertaken for the sole purpose of persuading the leaders of these countries to accept the proposals. Explaining the government's position on the Anglo-American proposal, Garba stated that: ". . . The document truly contained a number of the African demands in Southern Africa. Our demands like one man, one vote in those territories are contained in the proposals. In addition to one man, one vote, the document provided for a cease-fire; United Nations observers to monitor elections and activities of the police; a neutral transition administration with power over defense, law and order and electoral arrangements in the hands of an impartial administrator; integration of existing armed forces into one army that would be loyal to the elected government; and a democratic constitution with guarantees of individual rights for both black and white Zimbabweans.[13]

Obasanjo's trip to the front line states to drum up support for the Anglo-American proposals was one indication that the United States needed Nigeria's goodwill and support if its diplomatic initiatives in Africa were to succeed. Nigeria, on the other hand, needed United States cooperation in bringing pressures to bear against white minority rule in Southern Africa. Nigerian leaders realized that, not only was it almost impossible to go it alone, but political independence in Southern Africa could not be achieved through armed struggle alone.

The issue of political independence in Africa was of paramount importance to Nigeria. This stated foreign policy objective was consistently pursued under successive governments from Mohammed to Shagari. On December 2, 1975, the then Nigerian leader Brigadier Murtala Mohammed in an address to the Angolan people, said:

> We in Nigeria are committed to the total liberation of the whole of Africa and we will not fold our hands to see our brothers and sisters in Angola subjugated, exploited and recolonized by the racists and imperialists in South Africa and their supporters . . . your struggle is therefore our struggle and we will support you both morally and materially until absolute victory is gained in Angola.[14]

Muhammad was assassinated in 1976, and his successor, Olusegun Obasanjo made it clear that there would be no change in foreign policy objectives. In a speech marking Nigeria's 17th independence anniversary Obasanjo declared:

> . . . until all Africa is free, we remain unfree. . . . Nigeria will continue to support liberation movements in Africa until success is achieved. Any political process based on partial or total exclusion of large sections of the adult population, whatever the rationale, must crumble. When. . . . Namibia becomes free, when apartheid ceases to exist in South Africa, all Nigerians can hold their heads high.[15]

On several public forums Nigerian leaders expressed the nation's commitment to contribute her full quota to the liberation struggle in Africa. Nigeria's full quota was very substantial. In addition to the aid Nigeria gave to the freedom fighters through African Union, Nigeria also provided other direct bilateral military and economic aid to the tune of about $5 million a year during 1975–1980 to liberation movements in Southern Africa. Included in this aid package were small arms ammunitions and the services of C.130 Hercules military transport planes.[16] One highly publicized aid was the N13.5 million grants given to the MPLA government of Angola by Nigeria on December 20, 1975.[17] On July 5, 1976 at the meeting of African Union heads of state in Mauritania, Nigeria donated a quarter of a million dollars to the liberation committee to be used for the struggle in Zimbabwe.[18] In 1977 there was widespread discussion in government circles and the press in Nigeria about how far Nigeria could go on the issue of political change in Africa. The immediate cause of this discussion was the announcement by the Chief of Army Staff, Lt. General T.Y. Danjuma in June 1977 that Nigeria was ready to send troops to assist the liberation movements in Southern Africa. At best, Dajuma made propaganda mileage out of the announcement, for there was no evidence to suggest that such action was given any serious consideration by the Nigerian government. Although the military option was not given any serious consideration, Nigeria featured prominently in the discussion considered by some observers "to be the inevitable prospect of a direct military confrontation between black and white-dominated Africa."[19] Nigeria's reluctance to consider the military option was probably informed, in part by the realization that: if the future of Southern Africa was going to be determined militarily, it would be by a prolonged guerrilla war rather than through a direct military confrontation. However, Nigeria's military force can be reckoned with in the event of a confrontation between black and white-dominated Africa. A study by the International Institute for Strategic Studies concluded that Nigeria had "by far the largest and one of the best equipped forces in black Africa." Furthermore, the study showed that in 1978 Nigeria had an estimated total of 232,500 men, and spent $2.4 billion on defense. On the other hand, the study indicated that the strength of South Africa's defense forces was such that "she would be a match for any force which black African countries could assemble against her.[20]

The issue of political independence in Africa was very important to Nigeria. How sensitive was United States foreign policy to this issue? U.S. policy was based on the premise that Nigeria would remain a friendly country if United States foreign policy were sensitive to issues of great importance to Nigeria, particularly, the issue of "African emancipation. United States had attempted to carry out its pledge of cooperation with Nigeria in the cause of political independence in Africa by two means: economic/military assistance and diplomacy. The assumption here was that resources supporting a policy were key to its effectiveness.

Historically, United States official aid to Africa had been very small. From 1960 to 1976 Africa's share of United States aid averaged around 9 percent. By contrast, United States aid to Latin America was more than 20 percent. However, under the Carter administration more assistance was given than in the past. For example, United States aid budget for fiscal year 1978 included $460 million for Africa. This represented a 48 percent increase over 1977. In 1979 the Carter administration asked Congress for $294 million for the African Development Fund and $45 million for military assistance.[21] Nigeria was one of the several African countries which were beneficiaries of United States aid programs, having borrowed a total of $2 billion from the World Bank and American banks in 1978. In the Horn and in Southern Africa the United States made some efforts to help resolve disputes peacefully. In the Ogaden conflict between Somalia and Ethiopia, the United States urged all of the parties concerned to make efforts toward a peacefully settlement. During the Carter administration Assistant Secretary for African Affairs, Richard Moose visited Somalia. State Department reports on the trip indicated that discussions with the then Somalian President, Siad Barre were centered on: (a) obtaining assurances from President Barre that he "would respect the internationally recognized borders of his neighbors," and (b) informing the Somali leader that further United States aid to Somalia would be restricted in scope and "confined to defensive items only."[22] The implications here were that: (a) Somalia's respect for the internationally recognized borders of his neighbors would remove the causes of the Ogaden conflict, and (b) since the United States was the major arms suppliers to Somalia, a limited supply would have a halting effect on Somalia's ability to continue the conflict.

In Southern Africa the United States was an active member of the Contact Group, formed in April 1977 to find a peaceful solution to the Namibian question. United States chief negotiators, especially Donald F. McHenry during the Carter administration, at different points of the negotiation, came close to achieving a breakthrough. United States was instrumental in working out what became known as "the Contact Group proposal" for a Namibian settlement which included a call for "cease-fire, elections and independence for Namibia."[23] South Africa rejected this plan reportedly because it favored SWAPO's electoral chances. Kurt Waldheim, UN Secretary General at the time, warned in his report to the General Assembly in 1979 that such delay in freeing Namibia was "bound to lead to an escalation of violence and bring bloodshed and ruin to the region."

For decades, United States policy toward South Africa had been an ambivalent mixture: rhetorical condemnation of apartheid, sorrowful slaps on the wrist, and wishful thinking that contact and business would lead to evolutionary change, and revolution averted. Although Henry Kissinger had made a belated start in his Lusaka speech in 1976, the first real indication that change was imminent surfaced during the 1976 presidential election campaign when the Democratic Party charged that eight years of Republican administration's indifference, "accompanied by increasing cooperation with the racist regime, have left our influence and prestige in Africa at an historical low." In its place, the Democrats promised to "adopt policies that recognized the intrinsic importance of Africa, and the inevitability of majority rule" in South Africa. Furthermore, they promised to:

(1) Work aggressively to involve black Americans in Foreign policy positions. . . . And in decisions affecting African interests; (2) support majority rule in Southern Africa, recognizing that our true interests lie in peaceful progress towards a free South Africa for all South Africans, black and white; (3) lend support to African nations in denying recognition to 'Homelands' given pseudo-independence by the South African government under its current policy of 'separate development';(4) end relaxation of arms embargo against South Africa.[24]

The Carter administration attempted to fulfill some of these campaign promises by: (a) appointing Andrew Young as United States Ambassador to the United Nations; (b) having Vice President Walter Mondale handle the South African negotiations; and (c) by personally taking a direct interest in developing day-to-day policies towards Southern Africa. Furthermore, the administration took a number of actions to underscore United States' opposition to apartheid and racial discrimination in South Africa. One such action was to arrange a top-level meeting with the Vice President and South Africa's Prime Minister Mr. Vorster in Vienna in May 1977. The purpose of the meting was to inform Mr. Vorster that a new era had begun in United States-South Africa relations, and to warn him that, in President Carter's own words, "unless there is movement away from racial discrimination and separate development and toward full political participation for all South Africans, relations between our two countries can not improve."[25] United States supported the 1977 United Nations arms embargo against South Africa, and in 1978 imposed a ban on export of goods and technology to the South African regime.

Student Groups demanded that United States should do better and complained about the government's lack of political will and unwavering commitment to bring about change in South Africa. They called for stronger measures, including disinvestment and a trade boycott. Beyond diplomatic rhetoric United States did not do enough in the eyes of the some groups because of it's varied interest in South Africa. Nation states rarely pursue foreign policies that are not in their own interests. United States interests in South Africa went beyond the rhetoric of African freedom. What these interests were, Nigeria-United States perspectives on political change, and the common grounds that existed between both countries will be explored in chapter 3.

NOTES

1. OAU became African Union in 2001 when the African Economic Community and the Organization of African Unity were almagamated.

2. Address by the Prime Minister, *House of Representatives Debates*, 20 August 1960, and quoted by John Stremlau in *The International Politics of the Nigerian Civil War* (Princeton: Princeton University Press, 1977), 6.

3. John J. Stremlau, *The International Politics of the Nigerian Civil War* (Princeton: Princeton University Press, 1977), 5.

4. Quoted by Zdenek Cervenka, in *The Unfinished Quest for Unity: Africa and the O.A.U.* (New York: African Publishing Co., 1977), 14.

5. Akinyemi, "Nigerian Foreign Policy," 107.

6. John J. Stremlau, *The International Politics of the Nigerian Civil War*, 358.

7. Harold D. Nelson, *Nigeria: A Country Study* (Washington D.C.: American University Press, 1982), 225.

8. The Adedeji Report on Foreign Policy of 1976 recommended, among other things, that Nigeria adopt a militant foreign policy posture with some emphasis on the promotion and defense of the rights and interests of all black people.

9. President Ford urged the Nigerian leader not to recognize the O.A.U. meeting on the Angolan crisis. The letter provoked a bitter official verbal attack on the U.S. by Nigeria, which described the letter as an insult to Africa.

10. "Black Africa: More Weight in U.S. Policy Scales?," *Great Decisions* 1979, 54.

11. *National Security Council Strategy No. D18* (Washington, D.C.: U.S. Government Printing Office, 1978), 15.

12. *National Security Council* (Washington, D.C.: U.S. Government Printing Office, 1978), 15.

13. Colin Legum, *Africa Contemporary Records*, 1977–78 (New York: Africana Publishing Co., 1978), 59(C).

14. "Address by His Excellency Brigadier Murtala Muhammad to the People of Angola," *Nigeria: Bulletin on Foreign Affairs* vol. 5, n3 & 4, Aug–Dec., 1975, 89.

15. "We Must Sacrifice to Liberate Africa," *New Nigeria*, October 1977, 9.

16. Aluko, *Essays in Nigerian Foreign Policy*, 251.

17. "N13.5 Million Gift to Angola," *Nigeria: Bulletin on Foreign Affairs* vol. 5, n 3 & 4, Aug.–Dec., 1975, 3.

18. "Nigeria Donates to Liberation Committee," *Daily Times*, 6 July 1976, 9.

19. "The Military Equation: Black Africa Lags Behind," *Africa* vol. 82(N) (June 1978): 14.

20. *The Military Balance 1977–78*, International Institute for Strategic Studies, (London, 1978), 25. South Africa's armed forces were estimated to be 55,000 with an additional 90,000 in paramilitary units and spent an estimated $1.9 billion on defense.

21. Cyrus Vance, "Issues Facing the U.S. in Africa," *Department of State Bulletin* (July 1978): 29.

22. Vance, "Issues Facing the U.S. in Africa," 30.

23. For details see Legum, *Africa Contemporary Records*, C. 211.

24. *U.S. African Policy: the National Democratic Party Platform* (Washington, D.C.: U.S. Government Printing Office 1976), 5.

25. President Jimmy Carter, "Interview," *Africa Report*, (July–Aug. 1980): 8.

Chapter Three

Perspectives on Political Change in Africa

Nigeria and the United States were in agreement that political change in Africa was inevitable, but both countries disagreed on what political change meant, and how best to achieve it. However, the emphasis here is on the convergence of interests that existed between both countries on the issue of political change in Africa and their respective motivations.

NIGERIA'S PERSPECTIVE

Successive governments from Muhammad to Shagari saw it as "a duty to ensure that the wind of change blowing over the continent continues."[1] During the period covered by this study Nigeria's perspective on political change in Africa remained fairly consistent. Some of the elements of Nigeria's perspective useful for our examination of the issue of political change in Africa include:

1. Negotiated settlement. As evidenced by the country's support for United States initiatives in Africa, including the Anglo-American proposal, Nigeria supported change by peaceful means where feasible.
2. Armed struggle. Where negotiated settlement had failed, Nigeria expressed strong support for armed struggle for liberation movements in Africa.

In a policy statement made by General Muhammed in 1975, these two elements were implicitly echoed when he said "if persuasion failed, other methods would be employed." Obasanjo was more forceful in his approach. Speaking at

20

a White House dinner on October 11, 1977 he reiterated these two elements of Nigeria's perspective on political change when he expressed, on the one hand, "support for all efforts aimed at finding a just and peaceful solutions" to the issue of political change in Africa, and on the other hand talked about "his belief in the armed liberation struggle."[2]

The fact of change was perhaps more important to Nigeria than how change occurred. The same could not be said about the United States. On occasions, the United States had expressed concern about how change occurs and whose interests and influence it reflected. This has led to criticism that the United States was acting like the policemen of Africa, dedicated to preventing change. It should be pointed out that while Nigeria publicly embraced negotiated settlement and armed struggle, the United States publicly advocated only negotiated settlement. Although the United States had been known to be involved in several covert operations around the world that amounted to supporting armed struggle, it had fallen short of publicly adopting armed struggle as an official policy. This difference in policy did not preclude cooperation between both countries; it only led to minor irritations, with no major strain in relations. However, one could say that the United States was not necessarily against change per se, provided such change was not inimical to United States interests.

UNITED STATES' PERSPECTIVE

United States favored political change, but change brought about through negotiated settlement, and abhorred change brought about through armed struggle. Its strategy was to work with moderate African states in the cause of African emancipation. The U.S. was actively involved in peace initiatives in Africa including the Anglo-American proposal and the Brazzaville Protocol. Resolving these conflicts was seen in Washington as the best way to remove the opportunities for outside intervention in Africa.

The United States had the erroneous notion that countries experiencing political change in Africa brought about through armed struggle, aided by Russia, would as a matter of course, become Russian satellites. By interpreting events in Africa as a by-product of a global East-West conflict, the United States either ignored the nationalist dynamics of the African situation or was thoroughly ignorant of it. Thus, the United States on occasion, spoke out forcefully against armed struggle. And when tough talking failed, the United States invariably resorted to covert operations by secretly backing the opposing factions. For example, in 1975 after United States arm-twisting attempt to prevent African Union's recognition of the M.P.L.A. failed, it resorted to covert operation by secretly arming and funding the UNITA faction in Angola.

COMMON OBJECTIVE

It was obvious from both countries' perspectives that a common objective existed between them. That common objective was African freedom. This point was further highlighted by Obasanjo in a White House dinner speech when he reiterated that: "a close affinity already exists between our two countries. This affinity derives from our common attachment to freedom and independence."[3] Beginning with the Carter administration this common objective was recognized by United States policymakers. In a policy statement on June 7, 1978 President Carter stressed United States commitment to: "Africa that is free . . . free of dominance of outside powers, free of bitterness of racial injustice, free of conflict. . . ."[4]

However, at the beginning of the Reagan administration observers wondered if African concerns, such as the issue of political change in Africa, would be regarded as "high priority issues as they were in the Carter administration."[5] As it turned out, diplomatic rhetoric notwithstanding, the Reagan administration did not regard African concerns as high priority issues. To maintain the level of rhetoric, Reagan acknowledged the importance of the common objective existing between both countries, but did very little to back it up. Nigeria played a constructive leadership role in Africa, and cooperated with the United States in efforts to resolve some of the conflicts in Africa, but clearly both were not involved in these interactions for the same reasons. Officially, the United States expressed its preference for peaceful change, as opposed to armed liberation and its repercussions. According to Cyrus Vance, the United States preferred: Working for peaceful change. Violence bears many costs, in human terms, in a legacy of political polarization, in damage to economic interests and in the excuse it presents for outside interference.[6]

The idea of a peaceful change was sometimes difficult to pursue because of (1) the intransigence of the colonizers, (2) the successes of armed liberation struggle, (3) the continued flow of arms from Russia and other nations and (4) the presence of Cuban troops. The successes of armed liberation struggle were, to some extent, dependent on the level of arms flow from these countries and the presence of Cuban troops. In Ethiopia alone, Russia had flown in an estimated $2 billion worth of military hardware, 3,000 Russian military advisers and about 20,000 Cuban combat troops.[7] Similar efforts were duplicated in other African trouble spots, hence the concern expressed by the United States about Russia and Cuban activities in Africa. However, it was clear that the Cuban troops and Russian weapons were not the problem. The problem, was the existence of colonialism and oppression; white, minority-ruled governments pursuing discriminatory policies.

This became a source of disagreement between the two countries, with the United States linking the issue of Cuban troops with the question of independence; and Nigeria insisting the problem was not the Cuban troops but colonialism and oppression. In the words of Shagari, "linking the so-called issue of Cuban troops with the question of independence is as unjust as it is incomprehensible."[8]

The fact that both countries were not agreed on what the problem was in Southern Africa was a further testimony that the stakes for both countries in the liberation of Southern Africa were not the same. However, as has been indicated in our framework, disagreement in one area did not preclude cooperation in other areas.

Cooperation

Indeed both countries were actively engaged in some cooperative efforts in many of Africa's minor and major trouble spots.

Shaba

Nigeria's foreign minister, Joseph Garba's attempt to mediate the Shaba problem between Zaire and Angola in the summer of 1977, the peace efforts in Chad and Obasanjo's trip to the Frontline States were some of the positive indicators of these cooperative efforts between both nations to find solutions to some of Africa's pressing problems. Mention has been mad of Obasanjo's trip in the preceding chapter. Garba's mediation effort grew out of an understanding between him and Cyrus Vance. According to Donald B. Easum's testimony, the trade-off was that 'the United States would not overreact to the reported role of the Cubans" in the conflict.[9] Garba's trip was the first major step toward a peaceful settlement. It produced two meetings between the two countries in Brazzaville in July 1978. At these meetings both countries (Angola and Zaire) agreed to: (1) bring relations back to normal; (2) free the refugees in both countries, and (3) reopen the connecting railway line. This normalization was further consolidated by visits by both Heads of state. First, Angola's President Neto paid an official three-day visit at the invitation of President Mobutu on August 19, 1978. Second, the invitation for President Mobutu to visit Angola was contained in a joint Communiqué issued at the end of President Neto's visit to Zaire. In the communiqué both countries reaffirmed: (1) their respect for the aims and principles of the A.U. and the United Nations; (2) their pledge to establish a joint commission to increase security along their common border; and (3) their commitment to the development of close cooperation and the establishment of diplomatic relations.

Chad

Nigeria and the United States were actively involved in efforts to find a peaceful solution to the civil war in Chad. First, there was the initial peace effort spearheaded by Obasanjo and Shangari administrations that culminated in the well-acclaimed Lagos Accords.[10] Second, the collaborative effort between Nigeria and the United States on the Chadian crisis was first mentioned at the Cancun conference in Mexico where both leaders discussed the formation of a peace-keeping force to replace the Libyan forces in Chad. The inter-African peace-keeping force that was finally assembled from six African countries, including Nigeria, consisted of 5,000 troops, some 2,000 of them and the commanding general, General G.O. Ejiga, were from Nigeria. A substantial part of the cost for the Nigerian contingent was covered by the United States, having provided some logistical help and financial assistance to the tune of $12 million.[11] The functions of the peacekeeping force were to: (1) maintain law and order; (2) supervise elections, and (3) help in the integration of the Chadian army.

The idea of a peace-keeping force in Chad raised optimistic hopes when it was initiated. The move was seen "as an encouraging sign of some order coming out of the Chadian disorder."[12] Furthermore, it was in the interest of Nigeria and the United States to find a political solution to the Chadian crisis. Success in Chad would enhance Nigeria's credibility as regional power, and for the United States it would deprive Libya of a conflict to exploit. Thus, the similarity in both countries' position, and their cooperative efforts to reconcile the warring factions and work out a time-table for a ceasefire and elections were essentially in keeping with some of the elements of both countries' notions of their national interests. While there were similarities in both countries' perspectives on political change, the question remained were both countries motivated by the same interests?

MOTIVATION

As Richard Cottam puts it, motivation is a "compound of factors that predispose a government and people to move in a decisional direction in foreign affairs."[13] What was at stake for Nigeria and the United States in the liberation of Southern Africa? Clearly both were not motivated by the same interests.

Nigeria

Two important motivating factors for Nigeria were: moral obligation and commitment to African solidarity. There was evidence to suggest that Nige-

ria was motivated by its sincere commitment to the unfinished task of the total decolonization of Southern Africa. Nigeria saw this task as a moral obligation to assist fellow Africans who were still under colonialism. Successive
administrations since 1960 had consistently stressed the point that until all of
Africa was free, Nigeria will not be free. This expressed commitment to decolonization had also been backed by financial and logistical support for liberation movements in Southern Africa. The idea of black solidarity, as it relates to black people in the continent, was promoted by the Gowon
administration in a rather low-keyed fashion. However, under the Muham-
mad-Obasanjo administrations, black solidarity was raised to the front political burner. According to Aluko:

> It was raised to an important aspect of policy. Indeed, the Adedeji Report on for-
> eign policy in 1976 declared that one of the objectives of the country's external
> policy should be the defense and promotion of the rights and interests of all
> black people within and outside Africa.[14]

The Shagari administration had publicly emphasized this aspect of Nigeria's
foreign policy on several occasions. "The destiny of Nigeria," said Shagari,
"is inextricably linked with the fortunes of all the countries of Africa and all
the peoples of African descent abroad."[15]

Nigeria saw her role as Africa's spokesman, with a moral obligation to help
fellow Africans still under colonial rule to win their independence. As
Africa's most populous nation, with its relative wealth, it was understandable
that Nigeria spearheaded the cause of black people in Africa, particularly
Southern Africa.

United States

Critics asserted that the time had come to transcend the political rhetoric of
the United States in its so-called commitment to the cause of African emancipation; pointing out that there was more to the stated United States' position
than was readily discernible.[16] United States interests, they contended, were
not just Africa that was free per se, but free for the maintenance and or pursuance of United States' strategic and economic interests. Another factor was
the fear of the probable cut off of Nigerian oil. Strategic interests have generally included access to the region's mineral resources, security of Western
oil flows around the Cape and containing the spread of Russia and Cuban influence and military activities in Africa.[17] Specifically, United States' military
and strategic stake in Southern Africa was centered on the possibility of Russia access to naval bases in the region. Since the bulk of Western Europe's oil
supplies and a fifth of United States' pass through the Cape of Good Hope,[18]

a prolonged cut off of these supplies by Russia could wreak havoc on Western economies. Therefore, access to basing rights in Southern Africa was viewed by United States policymakers as giving Russia the military means to do so. David Rees summed up the strategic importance of the Cape route:

> For nearly two hundred years the critical strategic importance of the Cape to the Western trading system has been generally recognized. . . . In the age of the Cape Oil Route, the strategic significance of the best intermediary position between Europe and India is even further enhanced. . . . Consolidation of (Soviet) influence in South Africa would almost certainly be the penultimate stage in the economic strangulation of the West.[19]

Economic

The United States was heavily dependent on mineral imports form Southern Africa. These minerals were considered to be crucial to the production process of United States' industries. Four essential minerals: chromium, manganese, vanadium, and platinum gave the Southern African countries, particularly South Africa, their significance for the United States. Chromium and vanadium are vital to the production of anti-corrosive steels, and platinum is a major element in anti-pollution technology.[20] Table 3.1 shows the degree of United States import dependence.

Other aspects of United States economic interests are investments and trade. In 1980 United States investments in Southern Africa were estimated to be about $3 billion, with $2 billion of that in South Africa alone. South Africa dominated United States trade with Southern Africa. The breakdown is shown in Table 3.2. These figures partly explained why Southern Africa remained a major strategic and economic interest to the United States. It was conceivable

Table 3.1. U.S. Import Dependency on Southern Africa.

Mineral	% of Needs Imported	Major Southern Africa Supplier (% of U.S. Imports)
Chromium	90	South Africa (35)
Chromium	90	Zimbabwe (38)
Vanadium	36	Zimbabwe (20)
Antimony	52	South Africa (44)
Platinum Group	89	South Africa (42)
Manganese	98	South Africa (9
Industrial Diamonds	100	South Africa (81)
Cobalt	97	Zambia (7)

Source: U.S. Congress, Senate, Sub-Committee on African Affairs, "Imports of Minerals from Southern Africa by the United States and the OECD Countries," September 1980.

Table 3.2.   U.S. Trade with Southern Africa, 1978–1980.

	(Millions of Current U.S. $)					
	U.S. Exports to Southern Africa			U.S. Imports from Southern Africa		
Country	1978	1979	1980	1978	1979	1980
Angola	32	92	111	227	347	559
Botswana	2	6	6	63	61	89
Lesotho	5	5	8	—	—	—
Malawi	5	5	4	11	25	29
Mozambique	20	30	69	39	56	113
Swaziland	1	2	7	14	24	62
Tanzania	48	36	62	81	49	34
Zambia	44	68	99	116	125	205
Zimbabwe	1	1	19	—	—	42
South Africa	1,080	1,413	2,464	2,267	2,717	3,428
Namibia	10	10	14	5	6	4

Source: U.S. Department of Commerce, 1980.

that so long as there were no other overriding national interests, the United States would have simply continued its involvement in the region, irrespective of the political arrangement there. Furthermore, the United States had downplayed the strategic and economic aspects of its interest, while at the same time highlighting its stated commitment to the cause of African emancipation.

The Threat of Oil Weapon

United States dependence on foreign oil had significant implications for its foreign policy. In 1979 Nigeria provided 18.8 percent of United States oil imports, second only to purchases from Saudi Arabia. And it was estimated that United States investments in Nigeria in 1980 amounted to over $3.5 billion.[21] The bulk of these investments were in the oil industry, followed by investments in agriculture. The United States-Nigerian Joint Agricultural Consultative Committee was charged with the responsibility of supervising these investments in agriculture. The implication here was that Nigeria could use its oil as a leverage to pressure United States action on Southern Africa. The threat that Nigeria might cut off oil supply to the united States or nationalize United States investments to underscore its displeasure with United States policy in Southern Africa was probably credible, but United States policymakers would rather not face that prospect. Washington probably thought that Lagos was bluffing about the use of the oil weapon, but after a similar action was taken by Nigeria against Britain in1979[22] it was hard not to think that the threat was a credible one. Credibility could have been established in many ways. One method was through a declaratory statement of intentions. A second method was through consistent action. Nigeria's policy statement in 1979 that United States' recognition of the Internal Settlement regime in (Rhodesia) Zimbabwe will be met with "appropriate response" was interpreted to mean Nigeria would cut off United States' supplies of oil if the Muzorewa regime was recognized by the United States. Credibility is greatly enhanced if the threat is not out of proportion with the provocation[23] and there is evidence in the threatening nation's history to indicate that the threat may be actually carried out. It would appear that the oil cut off to United States was certainly not out of proportion to United States' non-support for Nigeria's Southern African policy, and Nigeria's action against Britain in 1979 seemed to have added to the credibility of the threat.

Gulf Oil Corporation got 60 percent of its oil from Nigeria, and when the United States Congress was debating, whether or not to lift sanctions against the Internal Settlement regime in (Rhodesia) Zimbabwe in 1979, a Gulf Oil representative told a congressional hearing that "we would not like to see our imports jeopardized by precipitous congressional action."[24] It was evident then that the Nigerian card was on the table, and Congress took note of it when it decided not to lift the sanctions if President Carter considered their retention to be "in the national interest." Their retention was, indeed, deemed by the President to have been in the national interest of the United States.

Could Nigeria have actually cut off the supply of oil to the United States? Nigerians felt very strongly about the situation in Southern Africa. Successive administrations, particularly from 1975, regarded the liberation of Southern Africa as a matter of high principle for which they were willing to pay whatever economic price. Therefore, under certain market conditions, Nigeria might have been tempted to take such action. At the height of the oil boom in 1979 Nigeria was being urged by a small but vocal sector of the Nigerian population to: (a) move from verbal protest to concrete action by organizing concerted economic reprisals against the West, particularly the United States, (b) cut off oil supplies to the United States, and (c) increase aid to frontline states and the liberation movements.[25] One important point to remember, however, was that oil sales represented about 80 percent of Nigeria's foreign exchange earnings. Thomas Schelling explained this paradox succinctly: "In threatening to hurt somebody if he misbehaves, it need not make a critical difference how much it would hurt you too—if you can make him believe that threat"[26] Thus, the implication here was that it did not really matter whether or not Nigeria lost revenue in the process, but that the United States was made to believe the threat. The point was to establish the credibility of the oil threat, which Nigeria succeeded in doing. Nigeria did not actually have to carry out the threat to obtain United States support for the cause of African emancipation; it only had to make the United States believe it. Nigeria, also managed to do that.

In sum, United States and Nigeria were not interested in the cause of African emancipation for the same reasons. While Nigeria was motivated by moral principles and its commitment to black solidarity, the Untied States was motivated by its strategic, and economic interests, and to some extent, the fear of the oil threat.

Shared perspectives had not really meant shared interests between both countries, but the real test of their perspectives on political change in Africa was in the problem areas of Southern Africa. In the following chapter, an attempt will be made to find out, on the basis of detailed empirical data, the actual positions taken by both countries on the issue of political change in Africa, using Angola, Zimbabwe, Namibia, and South Africa as case studies.

NOTES

1. *"Nigeria's Anxieties Over U.S. Policy,"* West Africa, 27 July 1981, 1688.

2. *Federal Ministry of Information Release No. 1466*, November 29, 1975, 3.

3. *Federal Ministry of Information Release No. 1466*, November 29, 1977, 2.

4. "Principal Elements of U.S. Policy," *State Department Bulletin*, Jelu 1978, 16.

5. For further discussions on Reagan's African Perspective, see Richard Deutsch, "Reagan and Africa," *Africa Report* (January–February 1981): 4.

6. C. Vance, "U.S. Relations with Africa," *State Department Bulletin*, August 1978, 11.

7. Colin Legum, "The Stakes in Africa," *Atlas World Press Review* (July 1978):16.

8. President Shagari, "Policy Toward Southern Africa," *An Address Presented at the Commonwealth Heads of Government Conference*, Melbourne, Australia, October 1981, 5.

9. "Nigerian-American Business Relations," Testimony delivered by Donald B. Easum before a *Hearing of the House of Representatives Sub-Committee on Africa* in Detroit, Michigan, April 29, 1981, U.S. Govt. Press, Washington, D.C.

10. In 1979 Nigeria brought all the warring factors in Chad to the conference table in an attempt to work out a peaceful solution acceptable to all. The resultant proposal that came to be known as the Lagos Accords was signed in Lagos on august 18, 1979.

11. "U.S.A.: Africa Policy Reflections," *Africa Confidential*, 6 January 1982, 4.

12. Alem Mezgebe, "Chad: The War Game," *New African*, January 1982, 10.

13. Richard W. Cottam, *Foreign Policy Motivation: A General Theory and Case Study* (Pittsburgh: University of Pittsburgh Press, 1977) 31.

14. Aluko, *Essays in Nigerian Foreign Policy*, 133.

15. President Shagari, *Address to the U.N. General Assembly* 6 October 1980, 5.

16. Pan-Africanists, including black Organizations such as the Congressional Black Caucus and university students across the U.S. held this view.

17. *The Report of the Study Commission on U.S. Policy Toward Southern Africa* (Los Angeles: University of California Press, 1981) 310.

18. *The Report of the Study Commission on U.S. Policy*, 318.

19. David Rees, "Soviet Penetration in Africa," *Conflict 77* (November 1976)1.

20. *Report of the Study Commission on U.S. Policy*, 310.

21. Aluko, *Essays in Nigerian Foreign Policy*, 138.

22. Following Mrs. Thatcher's statement of her intention to recognize the Muzorewa regime in (Rhodesia) Zimbabwe, Nigeria nationalized BP and disqualified British companies seeking contracts and licenses in Nigeria.

23. According to Kenneth Boulding, beyond a particular point, the higher the level of a threat, the lower the probability that it will be believed. See Kenneth Boulding, *Conflict and Defense: A General Theory* (New York: Harper and Row, 1962), 255.

24. Quoted by Richard Deutsch, "African Oil and U.S. Foreign Policy," *Africa Report* (September–October, 1979), 47–51.

25. Joseph Wayas, *Nigeria's Leadership Role in Africa* (London: MacMillan Press, 1979), 79.

26. Thomas Schelling, *Arms and Influence* (New Haven: Yale University Press, 1966), 36.

Chapter Four

Case Studies

The remarkable similarity in the political history of Angola, Zimbabwe, Namibia and South Africa was that they all suffered from some form of colonialism, oppression and the attendant effects of substantial white settlement. White settlement in these countries varied widely, however, from the long established white settlement in Angola dating back to 1575 and South Africa in 1652, to the much later colonization of Zimbabwe during the 1890s and Namibia in the early 1900s. Various theories were espoused by whites at different periods to justify their dominance: in Angola, the Portuguese fiction of assimilation and overseas provinces; in Zimbabwe, the white settlers' notion of "partnership"; in Namibia, the sacred trust; and in South Africa, the concept of apartheid. The major problem in all of these countries was essentially the same—that of protecting entrenched white minority interests while at the same time stifling the aspiration of the African majority.

Angola and Zimbabwe managed to shake the yoke of colonialism in 1975 and 1980 respectively, but not its ramifications; while Namibia and South Africa won their independence in 1990 and 1994. At one time or another the most important issue on the minds of Africans in these countries was the issue of political change. This chapter will examine how independence was won in these countries, with particular emphasis on the positions taken by Nigeria and the United States on the issue of political change in these countries.

ANGOLA

What was the political situation in Angola prior to the Portuguese collapse in 1975? How was the issue of political change settled, and what were the actual positions taken by Nigeria and the United States on this issue? A brief mention of Angola's colonial history is in order here. Portugal's colonial exploits in Africa dates back to the fifteenth century; and in the process, Portugal colonized a number of African countries including Angola, Guinea Bissau and Mozambique.[1] Historians assert that Portuguese explorers, led by Diego Cao, first landed in Angola in 1482, and Portugal effectively conquered Angola between 1575 and 1675.[2] After 500 years as a Portuguese Colony, Angola became independent on November 11, 1975.[3] According to Basil Davidson, "Europe's concert of imperial powers traced Angola's colonial frontiers as they are today."[4] Put simply, Angola was recognized as a colony of Portugal at the Berlin Conference of 1884–85. By 1925 Angola was effectively colonized by Portugal. Davidson's categorization seems to be the most useful. According to him, this task was accomplished in three phases. The first was up to about 1900, characterized by military invasion and the establishment of an effective presence by Portugal. The second, was during the early 1920s, and was characterized by pacification campaigns, which repressed African resistance. The third, beginning in the late 1920s until the 1950s, was concerned with the consolidation of Portuguese domination. Davidson declared that during Portuguese rule Angola's people were the "most deprived of any people anywhere":

> Angola's case is certainly extreme in its deprivation. . . . These people . . . lived in acute material distress and hunger. During the 1960s about 98 percent of all Angolans were completely illiterate, were denied any effective control over their own lives, and were unable to participate in any legal action to improve their lot.[5]

While the majority of Angolan people were economically deprived, Portugal was busy exploiting the Angolan natural resources for large profits for the metropolitan treasury. In defense of Portuguese colonialism in Africa, its statesmen used arguments similar to those that their predecessors had used for more than a century—"civilizing mission." The emphasis was placed upon the human and spiritual rather than material virtues of Portuguese colonialism.[6]

Africans were subjected to forced labor, and their lands expropriated. They were generally regarded as subhuman, people who would benefit from "white subjugation because of the opportunity it gave them for contact with a higher civilization."[7] The Portuguese forced labor system in Angola was widespread. It included "independent self-employed workers, women, children, the sick and the old." "Only the dead were really exempt from forced labor."[8] In 1942 African workers in Angola were paid $1.50 per month. And six years after the 1961 revolt, salaries of African workers had only risen to $3.00 per month.[9]

Legislation enacted by the Portuguese to systematically dispossess Africans of their land started in 1907 and continued through the early 1970s.

About 90 percent of the Africans in Angola lost their property rights as a result of the notorious decree No. 58470 of 1901 which was renewed in 1919.[10]

The alleged justification for Portuguese presence in Angola was to bring civilization to Africans. Yet more than 400 years later, the Portuguese were still treating the Africans as subhuman whose only value was as a resource of unpaid labor. By the time of the coup in 1974 Portugal had put in place a colonial policy that sought to protect entrenched Portuguese interests while at the same time perpetuating the inherent social and political inequality of the system by dividing the population into two separate classifications:[11] (a) indigena—uncivilized, unassimilated or natives. This category included nearly all Africans; (b) Nao-indigena—civilized. This included all whites and a small percentage of "blacks" considered civilized.

This extreme deprivation and exploitation was compounded by the lack of opportunity for political self-expression. Under these circumstances it was little wonder that a few hundred men, women and children decided to do something about it. They took to arms, and by the 1960s, independence movements that sprang up in Angola numbered well over a dozen.[12] Prominent among these was the Movimento Popular de Libertacao de Angola (MPLA: People's Movement for the Liberation of Angola) which launched armed struggle against colonial rule in February 1961,[13] in what has become known as the 1961 revolt. That year was, in the words of Irving Kaplan, "by any standard a watershed in Angolan history."[14] The revolt awakened the Portuguese out of their complacency and proved to Africans that they could turn their potential power into actual power. Portuguese attempt to suppress the liberation movements by force of arms led to widespread concern around the world, culminating in the detailed United Nations consideration of the situation in 1962. In January 19662 the United Nations General Assembly, after a debate, warned Portugal to cease repressive measures against the Angolan people. And on December 18, 1962 it voted 57–14 to condemn Portugal's colonial war against Angola.[15] An estimated 70,000 to 100,000 Portuguese troops were used in the savage military repression.

The liberation movements suffered a great deal from the reprisals of Portugal, but they were not completely destroyed. Despite the considerable amount of military support received by Portugal from NATO; by the late 1960s it was apparent to Portugal that a military solution to the issue of political change in Angola would not be in its favor. The alternative was predictable—the transfer of some power to some black elites in Angola. The problem was these elites did not represent the interests of the majority of the African population who regarded them as puppets. The election of these "puppets" to advisory legislatures in 1973 was a case in point, in that "real power" still remained in Portuguese hands. This cosmetic approach to political change did not address the real problems of Angola. Critics charged that the half-hearted reforms initiated by Portugal were deception schemes, an attempt by Portugal to minimize the gains of the liberation movements. G. Giovanni viewed the reforms in the same way Frantz Fanon, in *The Wretched of the Earth*, saw concessions granted by colonial powers, as an effective means of arousing a response of loyalty from the African people, consequently sabotaging the efforts of the liberation movements.[16]

There were a few half-hearted attempts at reforms geared toward equalizing the races before the law and legally discouraging racism. However, by the mid 1970s, the long history of Portuguese abuses against the African people, had turned into a military problem. Many in the military and in the civil service were convinced that the system was ripe for radical transformation. Thus, on April 25, 1974 a group of young military officers took over the government in a bloodless coup.[17] Observers contended that the immediate cause of the coup was the increasing military, economic and political pressures brought about by the high cost of Portugal's African wars. John Marcum gave a breakdown of the drain in Portugal's resources:

> Emigration soared to 170,000 in 1971, including a major outflow of draft-age men. . . 100,000 draft resisters left the country; there were fewer than one hundred cadets attending Portugal's four-hundred place military academy; and during the last call-up before the coup, some 50 percent refused to report. The toll in Portuguese military casualties . . . reached 11,000 dead and 30,000 wounded or disabled. Roughly 1.5 million Portuguese sought livelihoods abroad, leaving behind an internal workforce of just 3.5 million. The country ran a $400 million a year deficit, suffering Europe's highest rate of inflation (23 percent), and confronted mounting sabotage by anti-war underground movements unprecedented disciplined and effective.[18]

The coup speeded up the decolonization process which culminated in the Alvor Accord of January 15, 1975.[19] This independence agreement was signed by the Portuguese government and the three Angolan liberation movements. All the parties to the conflict pledged to work together in a coalition transitional government to govern Angola during the interim period to independence day which was scheduled for November 11, 1975. Observers saw this as a gamble from the outset. Predictably, it failed, and independence saw Angola engulfed in a civil war between the rival factions with MPLA eventually overcoming its rivals. At the time of the coup there were three major guerrilla movements and a few minor ones. The major ones were: The popular Movement for the Liberation of Angola (MPLA), led by Agostino Neto; The National front for the liberation of Angola (FNLA), led by Holden Roberto; and The National Union for the Total Independence of Angola

(UNITA), headed by Jonas Savimbi. Of the minor ones, the most important was the separatist-inspired Front for the Liberation of the Enclave of Cabinda (FLEC).[20] It appeared that the relative effective fighting strength, the primary objective of the movement and the chance of winning the elections were major factors in explaining why Nigeria and the United States supported a particular faction. But aside from these factors, there were several unspoken but critically important interests at stake for both countries in Angola. These will be explained later in this section. Of the three major guerilla movements, the FNLA was the major fighting force confronting the Portuguese at the time of the coup. Charles Ebinger, quoting official Portuguese estimates, put FNLA forces at about 2,000 "operating in the Dembos Mountains and an additional 10–12,000 guerrillas headquartered" on the Zairian side of the border, with additional scattered units elsewhere in northern Angola.[21] A breakdown of the movements' total forces is presented in Table 4.1.

In 1974 the MPLA's military prospects were very bleak, partly because: (a) it suffered from intense internal crisis; (b) it lacked operational base; and (c) it was never able to develop the military potential of its forces.

Finally, UNITA's prospects were also not impressive. Two major weaknesses were apparent: it was undermanned, and it lacked adequate supplies.

It was obvious that at the time of the coup none of the contending forces was strong enough to win without outside assistance. Since attempts by African governments and the African Union failed to find a solution to the Angolan problem non-African involvement became inevitable. The introduction of the external factor into the Angolan crisis changed the military equation. MPLA eventually won because of Cuban troops backed by massive Russian help in weapons and material.

The issue of political change in Angola was settled, not only by the liberation movements themselves, but with considerable help from forces outside Angola. These external forces and the roles they played in the Angolan crisis received considerable attention in the literature on foreign intervention in Africa. Let me now turn to an examination of the positions taken by Nigeria

Table 4.1. Movements' Total Forces.

Date	Movement	Number of Forces
January 1974	F.N.L.A	14,000
January 1974	F.L.E.C.	4,000
January 1974	U.N.I.T.A.	3,000
January 1974	M.P.L.A.	2,750
Total		23,750

Source: Marcum, *The Angolan Revolution*, vol. 2, 257.

and the United States in the Angolan crisis and analyze the motivations behind both countries' involvement in Angola.

Nigeria's Position

The Angolan crisis provided Nigeria with its first serious test in foreign policy during the period under study. The new government of Murtala Muhammad continued the Angolan policy of the previous administration which essentially was waiting to be part of an African consensus before stating Nigeria's position, while putting pressure on the three movements to form a National Government. It is important to note that until South Africa's intervention, the African Union maintained a broad consensus on its policy on Angola expressed as follows: (a) support for a Government of National Unity; (b) acceptance of MPLA, FNLA and UNITA as legitimate nationalist movements entitled to participate in such a government; (c) the maintenance of territorial integrity; and (d) opposition to all forms of foreign intervention.[22] When the prospect for a national government by the three movements failed, Nigeria's first stand was to favour support for UNITA and the A.U. line in favour of reconciliation and national unity in Angola. However, a few months later, Nigeria completely reversed this position at the AU emergency summit in Addis Ababa in January 1976. This "volte face" stemmed from the emergence of a new development: the open and direct military assistance which the South African regime was giving to the FNLA-UNITA alliance. South Africa's invasion of Angola on October 23, 1975 was cited as evidence of South Africa's involvement, which in Nigeria's view, had put a different complexion on the situation. In a communiqué issued on February 3, 1977 by the South African Defense Headquarters in Pretoria, South Africa admitted having given military assistance to the FNLA-UNITA coalition in September 1975, but insisted that the assistance was given on a "limited scale" only.[23] Whatever "limited scale" meant, there was no question about South Africa's involvement. Nigeria was convinced that there was abundant evidence of South African troops in the conflict. The factions fighting against MPLA were backed not only by South African but other interests which were clearly against Angolan independence and freedom. In a statement recognizing the MPLA as the legitimate government of Angola, the Nigerian leader, Murtala Muhammad, appealed to all Angolans to rally behind the MPLA. He pledged Nigeria's moral and material support until absolute victory was achieved. But why did Nigeria back UNITA in the first place? At first, UNITA was generally credited with the best prospect of emerging successfully should the October elections take place. Another rationale for Nigeria's support can be found in the report of a ten-member Commission of Enquiry set up by the AU which stated that "UNITA had the largest popular support" in Angola, followed by FNLA, and MPLA was a distant third.

It should be pointed out that Nigeria seemed to have adhered to its stated perspective on political change by: (a) working towards a negotiated settlement as demonstrated in its efforts to pressure the three liberation movements to cease hostilities and form a National Government; and (b) in a pragmatic move, showed support for UNITA because: (1) UNITA played the role of a mediator in order to bring about conditions conducive to holding elections, and (2) indications were that UNITA had a better chance of winning the election as a result of its strong popular support in Angola. Nigeria used the Angolan crisis to demonstrate its two-pronged perspectives on political change: negotiated settlement where feasible; armed struggle when necessary. Nigeria saw UNITA as a means to apply the latter.

United States Position

The Portuguese coup of 1974 made U.S. strategy in Angola grossly irrelevant; and the subsequent power struggle in Angola and its outcome exposed a basic flaw in the strategy. Through faulty intelligence, and a classic demonstration of how out of touch with the realities of the Angolan situation U.S. policy-makers were, Washington concluded that African liberation movements were ineffectual, not "realistic or supportable" alternatives to continued colonial rule. The "depth and permanence of black resolve" was questionable. As it turned out, the most inaccurate part of the conclusion was that "black victory at any stage" was completely ruled out.[24]

National Security Council study recommended some policy options for the United States in the region, including: (a) closer ties with white-minority regimes in the region, and (b) selective relaxation of United States' opposition toward the white-minority regime, and economic aid to the neighboring states. As it turned out, United States official policy became: (a) fostering closer ties with white-minority regimes, (b) adoption of a "lower profile" at the U.N., which meant softening criticisms of Portuguese colonial policy, and (c) $5 million in economic assistance for the neighboring states.[25] This study and the resultant policy ignored African interests and concerns in Angola. United States perception of the Angolan crisis as a test of big power rivalry with Russia, coupled with its strategic interest in Angola, seemed to have been the basic determinants of U.S. policy in Angola.

However, when the three liberation movements were attempting to settle the second phase of the issue of political change in Angola in 1975, the questions of "black resolve" and "black victory" were not the issues for U.S., policy-makers; rather, it was one of coming seriously to grips with what position to take and which faction to support. At a White House dinner for President Kenneth Kaunda of Zambia on April 19, 1975, President Ford declared the United States' position:

> We have been following developments in Southern Africa with great, great interest. For many years the United States has supported self-determination for peoples of that area, and we continue to do so today. We view the coming independence of Angola . . . with great satisfaction. . . . America stands ready to help . . . and to provide what assistance we can.[26]

For many years the United States had supported self-determination as it defined it, which invariably meant support for factions it considered to be "moderate" or pro-Western in orientation. In mid-July 1975 Secretary of State Henry A. Kissinger took the first major step towards actively involving the United States in Angola by requesting Congress "to vote a $79 million emergency aid program" supposedly for Zaire, but actually intended to provide arms for the FNLA-UNITA forces.[27]

United States had hoped that the Alvor Agreement would survive, leading to the emergence of a coalition government of national unity in Angola. According to Kissinger, in his testimony to the Senate's Africa subcommittee on January 29, 1976, the United States "have consistently advocated a government representing all three factions in Angola."[28] Once this hope was dashed, United States' immediate reaction was to support the FNLA-UNITA coalition. This support was given mainly through covert action. Press reports to this effect started to surface in early 1975 when "the National Security Council's 40 Committees authorized a covert American grant of $300,000 to the FNLA-UNITA factions."[29] The 40 Committee had outlined four options for the United States in Angola:

1. limited financial support for political activity;
2. substantial financial support and covert action, . . . costing $6 million;
3. larger amounts of money ($14 million) and material to give Savimbi and Roberto (FNLA-UNITA) superiority over Neto (MPLA); . . . and
4. sufficient support to sustain Roberto and Savimbi's (FNLA-UNITA) armies for a year, costing $40 million.[30]

By July 1975 the administration had stepped up its covert program to beef up the FNLA-UNITA forces. Reports in *Congressional Quarterly* indicated that between $25 to $50 million in military hardware was given to FNLA-UNITA by the end of 1975.[31] This turned out to be a conservative estimate, as the C.I.A.' s own estimate put the figure around a hundred million.[32] Edward A. Hawley, et al, lamenting this increased military aid to FNLA-UNITA wrote:

We are especially distressed at the rising level of United States involvement through. . . . Massively increased aid to FNLA-UNITA. . . . Such outside support can only prolong and intensify the fighting, strengthening those Angolans prepared to accept a neo-colonial pattern of independence and weakening those whose goals are true independence and self-determination.[33]

There were serious differences of opinion within the administration over the Angolan issue. At least, two view-points were discernible: (a) those who favored halting support for FNLA-UNITA; and (b) those who favored an increase in aid to FNLA-UNITA. Some top level officials in the State Department, including the then Head of the African Bureau, Nathaniel Davies, and both Houses of Congress were strongly opposed to continued United States support for FNLA-UNITA. These opponents were afraid of another Vietnam-type situation in Angola and stressed that claims that United States involvement would be limited was reminiscent of similar statements in the early stages of the Vietnam intervention. When the issue came to a head in December 1975, Congressional opposition was unmistakably made clear in a Senate vote of 54–22 to ban any further covert assistance to Angola.[34] The ban was sponsored by John V. Tunney (Democrat, California) as an amendment to the fiscal 1976 defense appropriations bill (HR 9861). And on January 27, 1976, the House of Representatives followed suit by voting 323 to 99 not to provide any further covert assistance to FNLA-UNITA forces.[35]

Prominent among those who favored increased aid to the FNLA-UNITA forces were the Secretary of State Henry Kissinger, United Nations envoy, Daniel P. Moynihan, and President Ford. Citing the issue of the Cuban presence and its policy implications for the United States, Kissinger argued his case before the Senate on January 29, 1976 without tangible results. The outcome in Angola, Kissinger warned, "will have repercussions throughout Africa." United States credibility in the region, he said, will be undermined if "(Soviet Union) and Cuba are unopposed in their attempt to impose a regime of their own choice in Angola." Kissinger not only argued his case for continued assistance for FNLA-UNITA, but defended his covert policy on the following grounds:

(1) We chose covert means because we wanted to keep our visibility to a minimum (2) we wanted the greatest possible opportunity for an African solution; (3) we felt that overt assistance would elaborate a formal doctrine justifying Great Power intervention-aside from the technical issues such as in what budgetary category this aid should be given; and how it could be reconciled with legislative restrictions against the transfer of U.S. arms by recipients; (4) the Angolan situation is of a type in which diplomacy without leverage is impotent, yet direct military confrontation would involve unnecessary risks; (5) thus it is precisely one of those grey areas where covert methods are crucial if we are to have any prospect of influencing certain events of potentially global importance.[36]

President Ford's letter to the House of Representatives on January 27, 1976 warning about the long term effect of the situation in Angola did not change too many minds either. The imposition of a military solution in Angola, the President warned, "will have the most profound long-range significance for the United States." Furthermore, the President declared that:

> The United States can not accept as a principle of international conduct that Cuban troops and Soviet arms can be used for a blatant intervention in local conflicts, in areas thousand of miles from Cuba and the "Soviet Union," and where neither can claim an historic national interest. If we do so we will send a message of irresolution not only to the leaders of African nations but to United States allies and friends throughout the world.[37]

It was estimated that United States military aid to FNLA-UNITA up to the time of MPLA victory was about $31 million, but the Select Committee on Intelligence of the United States House of Representative subsequently declared that the amount was much higher than that because of the covert nature of the operation and the use of secret CIA funds. The $100 million estimate seemed to have been a more realistic figure than any of the other quoted figures here.

Cool Relations

Nigeria-United States relations during Nixon-Ford administrations were decidedly cool. As a result, United States initiatives in Africa, particularly during the Angolan crisis, did not receive much support. Despite the lack of collaboration between both countries during the Angolan crisis both supported political change in Angola and efforts to find a peaceful solution to the crisis. For a while, Nigeria and the United States threw their support behind the same faction in the Angolan crisis, but for different reasons.

South Africa's intervention, which turned out to be a serious diplomatic and military miscalculation changed all that. This intervention destroyed the possibility of a collaborative effort between Nigeria and the United States and "all remaining hope of a unified African stance in opposition to outside intervention." Furthermore, South Africa's intervention was seen as a dangerous "American-South African collusion" which prompted African states such as Nigeria and Tanzania, previously critical of "Soviet" intervention," to rally "to the cause of the MPLA."[38] Kissinger has since denied this charge, saying: "Some charge that we have acted in collusion with South Africa. This is untrue. We have no knowledge of South Africa's intentions and in no way cooperated with it militarily.[39] Kissinger's disclaimer notwithstanding, United States collusion with South Africa was documented by the Senate Intelligence Committee in its 1978 report. The general conclusion was that South Africa entered Angola with the knowledge and approval of the United States. Why were Nigeria and the United States involved in Angola in the first place? What were the interests at stake for both countries?

Nigeria's Real Interest in Angola

Nigeria was involved in Angola to enhance its position as Africa's spokesman, dedicated to the liberation of Southern Africa. When peaceful negotiations failed, Nigeria shifted to a policy of active support for the MPLA and launched a vigorous campaign urging AU member states to recognize the MPLA at the AU summit meeting in Addis Ababa in 1976. Angola provided Nigeria with the first opportunity to demonstrate its stated commitment to black solidarity as it relates to black people on the continent. It is important to note that Nigeria's stand was directly opposed to that of the United States which had urged the members of the AU, including Nigeria, to oppose the MPLA and prevent its recognition at the AU summit meeting in 1976. Furthermore, Nigeria's stand on Angola effectively puts to rest the notion that resistance to Russian and Cuban activities in Angola was a matter of common concern to Nigeria and the Untied States.

U.S. Real Interests in Angola

Even when it was evident the MPLA was winning in Angola, United States adamantly stuck with the FNLA-UNITA faction. Thus it was clear that United States was involved in Angola, not to promote the cause of African emancipation per se, but to attempt to put in place a government that would protect its ideological and varied economic and strategic interests. Specifically, what were those interests? First, a word about United States method of intervention in general. Put simply, the standard method of United States intervention in third world countries was: (a) to identify in a troubled nation a local leader or faction considered moderate or pro-Western in orientation, and (b) supply this faction with military and material support to facilitate its victory over the opposing faction, ignoring the fact that this faction or leader might not represent the interest of his people. In Angola, the faction that fitted United States perception of a moderate, with pro-Western orientation was the FNLA-UNITA faction. United States funded and armed the FNLA-UNITA faction, not only during the war, but long after MPLA's victory in Angola.

Strategic Interests

United States strategic interests in Angola included the Azores Islands air and sea bases, the Lajes air base on Terceira and its backup field on Santa Maria

Island. In 1971 these bases took on added significance when United States signed an agreement with Portugal to extend United States "base rights through 1973" in return for a substantial aid package of over $400 million that included:

> $30 million in agricultural development assistance, (2) $5 million in drawing rights on U.S. Defense Department stocks of non-military equipment, and (3) eligibility for up to $400 million in Export-Import Bank financing for a variety of other development projects.[40]

These bases were crucial in redeployment of United States troops in Europe, particularly as NATO-related staging, refueling, and submarine tracking bases. In 1973 these bases were used by United States to rearm Israel in the Yom Kippur war.

Economic Interest

United States economic interests in Angola were centered around Angola's oil, diamonds, coffee and phosphates. United States companies acquired a significant control of the oil production in Cabinda province in 1966 and by 1975 Gulf Oil Corporation had invested more than $300 million in oil production and was pumping 150,000 barrels a day.[41] The Angolan port of Lobito was critical for imports from Angola and neighboring Zaire and Zambia. These imports included diamonds, copper, cobalt, coffee and phosphates destined for western markets.

Other Interests

Furthermore, Angola shared a common border with Namibia. This raised frequent concern in Washington that an MPLA government in Angola would serve as a springboard for the spread of communism to Namibia and elsewhere in the region.

Making Angola safe for the pursuance and maintenance of these interests, was the primary reason United States was involved in Angola. That United States had managed to cloak this in the political rhetoric of African freedom was perhaps an indication of the level of misinformation in the foreign policies of the big powers. After the independence of Angola, the focus of the Southern African liberation struggle shifted to Zimbabwe.

ZIMBABWE

Since the late 1800s Zimbabwe has had a troubled and violent political history.[42] Political scientists have generally examined the political history of

Zimbabwe under four headings:[43] (1) White Settlement; (2) Responsible Government; (3) The 1961 Constitution; and (4) The Unilateral Declaration of Independence (UDI).

White Settlement

Political scientists and historians have put the date of the arrival of the earliest white settlers in Zimbabwe at September 1890. These white settlers, who were known as Pioneer Column, numbered 200, and they were carefully recruited by Cecil Rhodes. After 1891 the anniversary of the arrival of the pioneer Column was celebrated as Occupation Day. In 1961 it was changed to Pioneer Day. Resistance from indigenous Africans to this occupation was met with ruthless force.

Responsible Government

The government that emerged from this illegal occupation collected the taxes, administered the country, and took on the full responsibility of government. In effect, Britain did not assume any real authority. In theory, it became a self-governing British colony after a referendum in 1923 in which the majority of the white population (59.4 percent) voted in favor of self-government. In practice, however, it enjoyed almost complete autonomy from 1890.

The 1961 Constitution

This constitution was a further attempt by the settler regime to make it impossible for Africans to effectively participate in the political system or achieve majority rule. The constitution created two voters' rolls, an A and B roll, with voting qualifications based on financial and educational standards that were out of the reach of most Africans. The implications of the new condition of franchise were that very few Africans could vote; and as a result, African demand for full political equality based on the principle of one man one vote was effectively rejected, while ensuring permanent white minority control.

The Unilateral Declaration of Independence (UDI)

The country's white minority government strongly resisted majority rule, and in order to ward off British half-hearted political pressure to bring about eventual democratic majority rule in Zimbabwe, the colonial government under Prime Minister Ian Smith issued on November 11, 1965 a unilateral declaration of independence (UDI), which purported to make the country an independent state, free of external control. Britain declared the country to be in a state of rebellion and invoked financial and economic sanctions, but refused to use military force against the Smith regime. From then until the Lancaster House Conference of 1979 the country was in an embattled state. The conference ultimately led to the independence of Zimbabwe in April 1980. This section attempts to: (a) isolate the problem in Zimbabwe; (b) show how the issue of political change was settled; (c) examine the roles played by Nigeria and the United States in settling the problem, and (d) highlight the real motivations behind both countries' position in Zimbabwe.

The Problem

An estimated 7,396,000 people lived in Zimbabwe in 1979. Of these, there were about 7,164,000 Africans; 11,000 Asians; 21,000 Coloreds; and 200,000 European settlers.[44] Beginning in 1890 the small body of European settlers, never totaling more than 5 percent of the total population, ruled Zimbabwe for 90 years. During this period the country was polarized between a dominant white minority and an oppressed, exploited African majority that were systematically excluded from effective political participation. How did this small white settlement dominate the African majority for 90 years? What was the response of the Africans?

Through a complex web of discriminatory legislations economic exploitation and the use of brutal force, the white minority managed to remain in power against the will of the majority. To understand the nature of the oppression and exploitation of the African majority, one should look at the conditions in which they lived. The objective material conditions of Africans in Zimbabwe under white settler regimes and the intransigence of these regimes made violent confrontation inevitable. Under the provisions of the Land Tenure Act of 1969, 50 percent of the land was reserved for whites. Whites took "those parts of the country having better soil and rainfall, and Africans were forcefully removed form their traditional fertile lands," driven to settle in the hot, unproductive, and at times, unhealthy parts of the country.[45] The average wage of the African in Zimbabwe was $190.60 a year while that of the white was $2,894. On education the government spent about $28 per African child in school per year as against $300 per white child.[46] Five years of education was the best most African children could expect.

Racism was legalized in a number of laws passed between the late 1920s and the early 1930s, "making race the determining factor for access to economic, political, and social privileges."[47] The country turned out to be one of privilege and ease for whites, while for the Africans it was one of subservience and frustration. African institutions were systematically destroyed, and their development aborted. What emerged out of this was a colonial system in which Africans were exploited as cheap labor, "separated from the white farms and urban centers either in reserves or segregated townships."[48]

The task of removing the political domination through which these conditions were being perpetuated gave rise to the emergence of guerilla movements in the 1950s. For Britain, and, to some extent, the international community, the problem was how to resolve the vexing contradiction of protecting entrenched white interests on the one hand, and providing equal opportunities for effective African political participation on the other hand. Until 1976 successive British governments, particularly since 1965, had failed to seriously address this problem. Predictably the country was headed for a bloody confrontation between the white settlers, who exclusively enjoyed political and economic power, and the African who had been systematically excluded from any effective political participation.

By making evolutionary change impossible, the settler regime made revolutionary change inevitable. Patrick O' Meara explained this point further:

> Not only was the white power structure unwilling to permit increased African participation, but it also limited channels of protest and opportunities for political mobilization. Ultimately, therefore, the nationalist moved outside of what they saw as a restricted political system.[49]

Moving outside the system meant waging a guerilla war against the white settler government, and when the war intensified in the 1970s several factions were vying for political power in Zimbabwe. The development of the guerrilla movement was very fluid, but four[50] notable factions were involved in the fight against the Smith regime: (1) Zimbabwe African People's Union (ZAPU). ZAPU was formed in 1961, and led by Joshua Nkomo; (2) Zimbabwe African National Union (ZANU), led by N. Sithole and R. Mugabe, was founded in 1963; (3) Front for the Liberation of Zimbabwe (FROLIZI), led by James Chikerema was formed in 1971, and (4) Zimbabwe Reformed African National Council (ZRANC), led by Thompson Tirivavi was founded in 1976. Intra-movement conflicts had sometimes been intense, but their fundamental objectives remained the same; (a) the wrestling of state power from the Smith regime; (b) the restructuring of the political system to permit the effective political participation of all Zimbabweans; and (c) the redistributing of the nation's wealth equitably. Wresting state power from the Smith regime required a prolonged guerrilla war that appeared unwinnable from Smith's standpoint, and its effect took its toll on the Smith regime.

Solution

The cost of the war in economic and human terms steadily rose, reaching a very high peak in 1978. Virtually all male Zimbabweans age 18–38 were conscripted. In February 1977 conscription was extended from age 38 to 50, and men over 50 were also encouraged to volunteer.[51] In economic terms the war cost the government over $1 million a day in direct outlay and several more millions in lost production. Morale was generally low as emigration reached a record level in 1978 In December of 1978 alone, 2,771 emigrated, and it was estimated that a total of 18,069 whites left in 1978.[52] A total of 14,149 left in the first nine months of 1979, and tourism, an important generator of foreign currency, dropped by 74 percent.[53]

In human terms it was estimated that more than 8,000 people, mostly civilians, had died and several thousand were wounded. A 10 percent income tax was imposed in 1975.[54] Under these circumstances the Smith regime had no alternative but to make peace.

The Anglo–American Proposals

Several attempts were made beginning in 1965 to find a peaceful solution to the Zimbabwean crisis. All these attempts made by successive British governments, Labor and Conservative alike, were doomed primarily because independence was to be granted under white minority rule, with only token African political participation. Only after a Untied States initiative, spearheaded by Henry Kissinger, which was designed to bring about majority rule in Zimbabwe surfaced in March 1976, did the British government concede for the first time that majority rule was indeed its objective. Thus, for the first time since 1965 the British objective appeared to converge with that of Nigeria and the United States on the issue of political change in Zimbabwe.

The Roles Played by Nigeria and the United States

What were the essential elements of the Anglo-American Proposal? How instrumental was it in bringing about political change in Zimbabwe? What were the actual positions taken by Nigeria and the United States on the issue of political change in Zimbabwe? It is important to note that the Kissinger initiative, the Anglo-American Proposals and the Lancaster House Agreement were belated responses to the call made by the African Union in the Lusaka Manifesto of 1969.[55] In this document, the AU: (a) warned of the threat to international peace and security brought about by misunderstandings and conflict of interest among nations; (b) appealed to the international community for cooperation in achieving peaceful change in white minority ruled territories; (c) stated its objectives in these areas; and (d) declared its preference for negotiated settlement.[56] The Lusaka signatories, while asserting their preference for peaceful change or negotiated settlement, also indicated that they would not hesitate to support armed liberation struggle if necessary. They summed up their position as follows:

> We would prefer to negotiate rather than destroy, to talk rather than to kill. We do not advocate violence; we advocate an end to the violence against human dignity which is now being perpetrated by the oppressors of Africa. If peaceful progress to emancipation were possible, we would urge our brothers in the resistance movements to use peaceful methods of struggle even at the cost of some compromise on the timing of change. But while peaceful progress is blocked by actions of those at present in power in the states of Southern Africa, we have no choice but to give to the peoples of those territories all the support of which we are capable in their struggle against their oppressors.[57]

Kissinger's response to the Lusaka Manifesto was contained in his own Lusaka Declaration of April 25, 1976 in which he accepted the AU proposals and reaffirmed:

> . . . . . . the unequivocal commitment of the United States to human rights, as expressed in the principles of the United Nations Charter and the Universal Declaration of Human Rights. We support self-determination, majority rule, equal rights and human dignity for all the peoples of Southern Africa-in the name of moral principle, international law and world peace[58]

Several developments in Southern Africa forced the United States to rethink its policy. One of them was the success of armed struggle in Guinea Bissau (1973), Mozambique (1975) and Angola in 1975. Another significant development was the presence of Cuban and Russian forces in Angola. MPLA victory in Angola was interpreted as a serious blow to United States credibility as a global power. United States had to salvage its credibility by playing a constructive role in the process of political change in Africa. It was against this background that Kissinger made a belated response to the Lusaka Manifesto seven years later.

However, it opened the way for some major diplomatic initiatives in 1977 by the Western powers: (a) The Anglo-American Proposals in Zimbabwe; (b) the mediation effort in Namibia by the Western powers (Contact Group); and (c) a renewed focus on the South African problem. The last two initiatives are discussed elsewhere in this study. Before a coherent policy could be developed out of these initiatives, a new administration came into office in the United States, and Dr. Owen was appointed as the new Foreign Secretary in Britain. Following up on the Kissinger initiative, the new administration of

Jimmy Carter launched a joint peace initiative in March 1977. New proposals for a settlement were published in a British white paper on September 1, 1977.[59] This document, known as the Anglo-American Proposals contained some essential elements for a peaceful and irreversible transfer of power to black majority rule in Zimbabwe. These essential elements included: (1) the abdication of the Smith regime; (2) a British resident commissioner to preside over the transition; (3) a new constitution guaranteeing majority rule and minority rights; (4) internationally supervised elections based on one man, one vote; (5) integration of existing armed forces into one army that would be loyal to the elected government; and (6) an internationally financed aid program for an independent Zimbabwe.[60]

To minimize objections to this plan, close consultations were held with Nigeria and the Front Line States (Tanzania, Zambia, Mozambique, Botswana and Angola) in its planning and implementation. In September 1977 General Obsanjo came out very strongly in support of the Anglo-American Proposals. In his tour of the front line states in September 1977 to drum up support for the proposals, Obsanjo declared in Lusaka, Zambia that the document "is a positive step towards majority rule in the territory," insisting that "it should be given a chance."[61] In Zaire, Obasanjo confirmed that "Britain and the United States had jointly given Nigeria and other African countries concerned the assurance of their determination to work with African countries to achieve majority rule in Zimbabwe."[62]

The four months between September 1977 when the Anglo-American Proposals were published and January 1978 turned out to be crucial in three respects: (a) during this period the Patriotic Front was struggling with its own deep internal divisions and was unable to reach agreement on some of the key aspects of the plan; (b) while Britain, Nigeria and the United States were busy attempting to sell the plan to the front line states and the international community, the Smith regime saw an opportunity to devise an alternative plan; and (c) on February 15, 1978 the Smith regime announced the successful conclusion of the "Internal Settlement" negotiations.

The Internal Settlement

On March 3, 1978 the Smith regime signed an agreement with moderate African factions led by Bishop Muzorewa. Under the new constitution the 212,000 whites still maintained their special status. Although they constituted only about four percent of the population, they were guaranteed 28 of the 100 seats in parliament. Furthermore, for ten years they would have controlled through a complex veto provision the judiciary, the civil service and the security forces.[63]

The Patriotic Front rejected the internal settlement on the grounds that it preserved the existing structure of the state in that: (a) black leaders were simply taking over some of the apparatus; (b) real power still remained in the hands of the white minority; and (c) no redistribution of the nations wealth was undertaken. In his assessment of the internal settlement Robert Mugabe said:

> All that has happened is a change of heads- a black head being substituted for a white but with the body still the same- the same armed forces, the same civil service, the same judiciary, the same economic structure . . . a head acting as a megaphone.[64]

Observers described the internal settlement as a means "to perpetuate the racial division which has brought 'Rhodesia' to its present wretched state."[65]

The United Nations Security Council adopted a resolution on March 15, 1978 which described the internal settlement as "illegal and unacceptable."[66] In defense of the internal settlement the new Prime Minister Bishop Muzorewa declared that:

> I do not want this new country to be a sham, a fraud, a hollow shell with the mere trappings of independence—a brand new flag, sleek limousines, black faces in parliament and the U.N. I do not want Zimbabwe ever to become another banana republic.[67]

Muzorewa must have been listening to his critics because those were the exact words used to describe the internal settlement—sham and fraud. Others called it a sell out.[68] However, Bishop Muzorewa was officially sworn in as the first black Prime Minister on May 29, 1979 after winning the April elections.[69]

While the internal settlement and the new government of Prime Minister Muzorewa were generally rejected and ignored by those who sought a credible black majority rule in Zimbabwe, observers noted that the internal settlement was perhaps the beginning of a significant change. A sharp decline of white power was envisaged. The decline was reflected in the views of Ian Smith, the architect of white supremacist rule, when he said he "was compelled to concede that the basic reason for the Unilateral Declaration of Independence (UDI) on November 11, 1965 was no longer tenable."[70] Furthermore, Smith was quoted as saying in *Time* magazine that:

> Whether we like it or not minority governments are unacceptable to the rest of the world. I had always hoped we could avoid black majority rule in my life time. But you have to change your tactics in this game, and we came to the conclusion that if we did not change, we couldn't survive.[71]

Several months after the institution of the Muzorewa regime, the three major questions facing the country were still unsettled: (a) ending the war; (b) removing economic sanctions; and (c) gaining international recognition. The Patriotic Front saw nothing to be gained from talks with the Muzorewa regime. Instead, it intensified the war efforts by successfully establishing larger numbers of guerrilla forces inside Zimbabwe. The turning point of the war came perhaps in September 1978 when a Viscount aircraft of Air Rhodesia was shot down by guerrilla forces, killing most of the passengers. By mid 1979 the weaknesses of the transition government produced fears and frustrations in the country. Several major incidents in the guerrilla war, such as the second Air 'Rhodesia' Viscount aircraft that was shot down on February 12, 1979, killing all the 59 people on board, heightened the fears and frustrations of the white population of Zimbabwe.[72]

At this point in the conflict the thrust of the Anglo-American initiative was to bring all the factions in the internal settlement and the external movement to an all party conference. However, before any progress could be made in this direction, two events occurred which had a negative impact: First, the conservative party had won the April elections in Britain and Margaret Thatcher had pledged in her campaign to recognize the Muzorewa regime and lift sanctions. Signaling her intentions, Mrs. Thatcher said at a press conference in Canberra, Australia on July 1st, 1979 that she would not try to get Parliament to reimpose sanctions and that recognition "might take a little longer."[73] A few days later, Lord Carrington, British Foreign Minister, was reported to have told Moraji Desai, the then Indian Prime Minister, that the British government would "formally recognize the Muzorewa regime" soon after the Commonwealth Conference, that year.[74] Second, the United States Senate, in one of its several attempts to undermine White House policy on Zimbabwe, voted 75 to 10 on May 15, 1979 to recommend the lifting of sanctions.[75]

As the Commonwealth Conference in August 1979 approached, there were increased speculations that the British government would announce its recognition of the Muzorewa government soon after the summit. The attempt by Prime Minister Thatcher and some Republican Congressmen headed by Senator Jess Helms to recognize the Muzorewa regime and lift sanctions was blocked by pressures from Nigeria and the Carter administration, especially the Africanist Group in the Carter administration. The Nigerian government, in one of its many messages to the Thatcher government, on June 5, 1979 insisted that any attempt to recognize the Muzorewa regime would amount to "provocation and a calculated and deliberate spite, constituting a wanton disregard for African opinion and well-being and deserving of an appropriate response."[76] Also the Carter administration expressed deep concern that Britain's intention to lift sanctions would be counterproductive. Ambassador Donald McHenry argued that Britain was "on a very wrong course by not referring the issue of sanctions to the Security Council."[77]

As delegates from 39 Commonwealth Countries were preparing to gather in Lusaka from August 1–7, 1979, the British press supported Britain's position and recognition of the Muzorewa regime. The *Economist*, in its editorial of May 26, 1979 called on Mrs. Thatcher to recognize the Muzorewa regime; and predicted that Nigeria would "only bark and not bite."[78] *The Daily Telegraph*, on June 14, 1979 also urged the British government to recognize the Muzorewa regime and present the Commonwealth Conference with a fait accompli.[79] It was against this background that Nigeria responded on the opening day of the conference that it was confiscating the assets of British Petroleum (BP) in Nigeria. The implications of this action included a loss of BP's entitlement to about 300,000 barrels a day of Nigerian oil and its 40 percent interest in the Port Harcourt oil refinery.[80]

Britain drew the proper lesson from this action and Mrs. Thatcher departed significantly from her Canberra statement when she later said that her administration "is wholly committed to genuine black majority rule in Zimbabwe, " and added that the aim of her administration "is to bring Zimbabwe to legal independence on a basis which the Commonwealth and the international community as a whole will find acceptable."[81]

Several issues were discussed at the conference,[82] but the resolution of the Zimbabwean problem attracted considerable attention. On this issue there was a meeting of minds—that what was needed was a peace plan acceptable to all parties to the conflict. This consensus was reflected in the final Communiqué[83] of the conference in which the Heads of Government agreed, inter alia, on the following objectives: (a) genuine black majority rule; (b) the effective participation of "all parties to the conflict" in the peace process; (c) a democratic constitution including "appropriate safeguards for minorities"; (d) a free and fair election supervised under British government authority; and (e) the presence of a commonwealth observers team to monitor the election.

There were mixed reactions[84] to the outcome of the meeting, but as it turned out, a giant step toward the resolution of the Zimbabwean conflict had been taken. The Lusaka Agreement laid the basis for what finally emerged from the Lancaster House Conference.

The Lancaster House Conference

One of the remarkable things about the Lancaster House Conference was that the rival sides to the conflict were brought to the same negotiating table, which was one of the objectives of the original Anglo-American initiative. When the conference opened on September 10, 1979, several key issues were addressed: (a) an internationally acceptable constitution, (b) conditions for a ceasefire, (c) the supervision of the elections, (d) the land issue, and (e) the status of the Patriotic Front's guerilla forces during the transition period.[85] Early in the negotiations. Muzorewa agreed to the need for a fresh election, which effectively meant relinquishing his office for a truly independent Zimbabwe. On the other hand, the Patriotic Front had initially insisted on United Nations-supervised elections, as opposed to British-supervised elections, but dropped its opposition after President Nyerere's personal intervention. Thus, the major point became the function and composition of the Commonwealth monitoring force. With some persuasion from Nigeria and the front line states, Britain agreed to a plan that called for: (a) a civilian group to observe the elections; and (b) the formation of a Commonwealth force to monitor but not enforce ceasefire. Land redistribution was already agreed upon, but several questions were raised such as (a) who would provide the money for compensation to be paid to the farmers, and (b) who would be affected by redistribution? A timely intervention by the United States saved the talks. President Carter promised a substantial contribution toward a land compensation fund,[86] thus, initiating a multi-donor program that later attracted donations from other countries including Britain and Nigeria. On the status of the guerilla forces during the transition period, the plan recognized the Patriotic Front's guerillas on an equal basis with that of the Muzorewa regime. With these key issues resolved, the conference closed on a rather positive note on December 15, 1979. The final agreement, known as the Lancaster House Agreement, was signed by both parties to the internal settlement and the external movements on December 21, 1979. In essence both parties agreed to: (a) observe a ceasefire, monitored by Commonwealth Forces; (b) accept the outcome of a British-supervised and internationally observed elections to be held after a two-month transition period.[87] In the meantime, Britain assumed control over its "rebel" colony Rhodesia on December 12, lifted sanctions and installed Lord Soames as the British governor.[88] Thus, the end had come to Ian Smith's illegal regime, and the results of the elections that followed confirmed even Smith's own belated admission that minority regimes "are unacceptable" to Zimbabweans.

Robert Mugabe's faction of the dissolved Patriotic Front won the elections of February 1980 in a landslide[89] and went on to form a coalition government with Joshua Nkomo's faction in March 1980; thus, finally settling the issue of political change in Zimbabwe. Nigeria and the United States were given part of the credit for this desirable outcome. However, perhaps the critical factor was the success of the liberation movements on the battle field.

Improved Relations

Nigeria-United States relations during this period witnessed a dramatic turn around from the open differences over the Angolan crisis and Nigeria's subsequent refusal to admit Kissinger into the country, to cordial exchanges and cooperation which culminated in state visits by the leaders of both countries.[90] This positive turn in relations was attributed to a number of factors including: (a) President Carter's stated commitment to the cause of African emancipation, based partly on his emphasis on human rights, (b) Nigeria's oil export to the United States and U.S. investment in Nigeria, and (c) U.S. willingness to de-emphasize East-West confrontation in Africa.

Nigeria supported the Anglo-American proposals, and Obasanjo undertook a trip to the Front Line states to drum up support for them. Andrew Young also received part of the credit for this because of "his influence on American policy in Africa and the close consultations initiated with Nigeria" over Southern African issues.[91]

Cooperation

And when it was clear that the Thatcher government and the conservative elements in U.S. Congress were leaning toward recognizing the Muzorewa regime, the Obasanjo and Carter administrations resisted Britain and congress, respectively. Both countries were active participants in the Lancaster House Conference. They both played constructive roles at critical points of the talks by helping to avoid a breakdown over the land issue and questions concerning the monitoring force. All of this occurred at a time the Patriotic Front was clearly winning the war. What were the motivating factors behind both countries' involvement in Zimbabwe? Were there some areas of common interest in Zimbabwe?

Motivating Factors

Nigeria

Two factors can be identified: (a) Success in Angola, and (b) the oil wealth. Success in Angola seemed to have elevated Nigeria's Southern African crusade to new heights. The crusade was intensified on many fronts: (a) economic reprisals were taken against Britain, (b) increased moral and material support were given to liberation movements, and (c) Nigeria took a more active role in the negotiation process. A friendly administration in Washington, coupled with the new oil wealth, meant that Nigeria was prepared to consolidate its position as Africa's spokesman, committed to the liberation of Southern Africa.

United States

Although United States had other interests in Zimbabwe, African concerns and interests also played a role in its involvement in Zimbabwe. The Carter administration's approach to the situation in Zimbabwe represented a significant departure from the approach of the Nixon-Ford era in that African concerns and interests were regarded as high priority issues. This approach rested on sound premises that included, among others: (a) fundamental change in Southern Africa was not necessarily inimical to United States interests, and (b) the best way to protect and promote Untied States interests was for the United States to identify itself as a friend of Africa, sympathetic to the aspirations of the African people.

Other Interests

(1) Credibility: The United States was involved in Zimbabwe partly to salvage what was left of its already shaken credibility in the region. MPLA's victory in Angola was interpreted by policymakers in the United States as a serious blow to U.S. credibility as an honest broker in the region. Kissinger warned in 1976 that the lack of a direct U.S. response to Russia in Angola would translate into a substantial loss of credibility for the U.S. in the region. Thus, to preempt further Russian influence and activities in the region, the U.S. became actively involved in efforts to find a solution to the situation in Zimbabwe. It was in this context that United States not only claimed credit for the outcome in Zimbabwe, but concluded that the outcome in Zimbabwe enhanced U.S. credibility as a global power, and at the same time, it deprived Russia of a conflict to exploit.

Strategic Minerals

Some of the major minerals that make Southern Africa vital to the United States are found in Zimbabwe. Two of these minerals are chromium and vanadium. They are vital to the production of anti-corrosive steels. Other minerals found in Zimbabwe include asbestos, magnesium, phosphates, and uranium.[92] Union Carbide had a profitable investment in chrome mining and smelting in Zimbabwe. It was estimated that United States had the third highest foreign investment in Zimbabwe, about 20 percent of the total foreign investment, with South Africa and Britain first and second, respectively. United States importation of chromium had jumped form 10.2 percent in 1974 to 38 percent by 1980, despite a United Nations embargo.[93]

It would appear that U.S. policy-makers had correctly interpreted events in Zimbabwe and concluded that an African victory was inevitable. Therefore, in order to enhance its credibility in the region and protect its varied economic interests in the long run, the U.S. had to play a constructive role in finding a solution to the problem in Zimbabwe.

NAMIBIA

Namibia's relatively short recorded political history can roughly be examined in three parts: (1) the German Era, (2) the Mandate Era, (3) the Post Mandate Era.

The German Era

At the Berlin Conference of 1884–5 Africa was partitioned among the imperialists. Germany took Namibia, known then as (South West Africa) and forced the indigenous Africans in the territory to sign treaties effectively giving up their sovereignty. With Germany's imperial control established, a systematic looting of the resources followed. By the end of the century Germany had "seized by legal trickery, guile or force much of the best land and cattle" in Namibia. African resistance was met by an extermination order issued by General Von Trotha. A Blue Book published in 1918 documented some of the atrocities committed by Germany during this period.[94] During World War I, colonialism in Namibia changed hands.

The Mandate Era

South Africa invaded the territory in 1915, and would have taken over Namibia as its fifth province at the end of the war if U.S. President Woodrow Wilson had allowed it.[95] Instead, under Article 22 of the League of Nations Covenant Namibia became a Class "C" mandated territory administered by South Africa on behalf of the League of Nations. In President Wilson's terms, the territory was entrusted to South Africa as "a sacred trust of civilization, to promote to the utmost the material and moral welfare and the social progress" of the Namibian people.[96] South African atrocities in Namibia were on a larger scale than those of the Germans. Africans were used as cheap labor, and relegated to inadequate, poor-quality native reserves. African resistance was met by bombings of "their women and children." The Africans quickly learned that they had exchanged an overseas tyrant for one from next door.

Upon the formal dissolution of the League of Nations in April 1946, all former mandates not granted independence were placed under Untied Nations trusteeship. But south Africa refused to either grant Namibia independence or place it under the United Nations trusteeship system. instead, South Africa sought permission to annex the territory. Furthermore, South Africa discontinued its annual reports on Namibia and refused to send petitions from the Namibian people to the United Nations. From then on, independent African states, with lukewarm support from the United Nations took on the task to settle two crucial problems: (a) the status of Namibia, and (b) political change in the territory. The rulings of the International Court of Justice did little to resolve these problems. In July 1950 the Court rendered an opinion on the international status of Namibia. It advised, inter alia, that: South Africa's obligations under the original mandate continued and that it was not mandatory that South Africa should place Namibia under the United Nations trusteeship system.[97] In an attempt to lay the groundwork for eventual independence for Namibia, Ethiopia and Liberia went to the Court once again in 1960. They charged, inter alia, that South Africa had: extended apartheid to Namibia and violated the human rights of the Namibian people and prevented progress toward independence.[98] After six years of arguments and one interim decision in which the Court ruled that Ethiopia and Liberia, both former members of the League, had the right to file the charges, the Court in July 1966 reversed itself and concluded that the two complainants had no status to bring the proceedings.[99] Thus, by ruling on the procedural and not the substantive aspect of the case, the Court hindered the efforts of those who were seeking to achieve independence for Namibia and strengthened South Africa's intransigence.

Post-Mandate Era

The Court's ruling was greeted with anger and dismay by concerned African states in particular, and the General Assembly in general. Thus, on October 27, 1966 the General Assembly voted 114 to 2 to adopt resolution 2145 which revoked South Africa's mandate, formally removing Namibia from South African control.[100] Furthermore, the resolution made South Africa's presence in the territory an illegal occupation. Under this resolution Namibia was to become the direct responsibility of the international community charged with the task of brining the territory to independence. Successive South African governments had defied the United Nations before revocation of the mandate, and insisted that with the demise of the League, all their international obligations regarding the mandate lapsed.

The need to remove this illegal occupation that had lasted for over 51 years in utter defiance of the wishes of the Namibian people and the United Nations gave rise to the emergence of several liberation movements in Namibia.[101] The most important movement was South West African Peoples Organization of Namibia (SWAPO) led by Sam Nujoma. SWAPO was recognized by the United Nations and most of the world as the legitimate representative of the

Namibian people. Since its formal inception in 1960 SWAPO spearheaded the liberation struggle against South Africa's illegal occupation. Sam Nujoma urged "all Namibian patriots to maintain unity, vigilance and intensify at all fronts in the struggle for the national liberation of Namibia."[102] Nujoma's call notwithstanding, South Africa's illegal regime was enforced and perpetuated by all the massive apparatus of apartheid law, military occupation, judicial rulings, a nationwide and ruthless police establishment, and total economic exploitation of the African population.

With Zimbabwe's independence in April 1980, the focus of the international community centered on Namibia. Namibia was thought to be next. But such optimism was replaced by cautious speculation. However, one thing seemed certain: political change in Namibia was inevitable. What was not certain was how political change in Namibia would be achieved. Would it be through negotiated settlement or armed struggle or both? We shall examine the efforts of the international community, with particular emphasis on the positions taken by Nigeria and the United States, to resolve the Namibian dispute.

Kissinger's Lusaka Declaration of 1976 marked the beginning of new attempts to resolve the Namibian dispute. Part of that speech dealt with the Namibian question in which Kissinger outlined United States position. He reiterated U.S. call for full political participation for all Namibians, urged the South African government to set a definite date for Namibian independence, restated U.S. commitment to work with African leaders to achieve the goal of independence for Namibia, and promised to provide "economic and technical assistance to help Namibia take its rightful place among the independent nations of the world.[103] This policy outline, coupled with Carter's commitment to human rights, opened the way for subsequent mediation efforts by the Western nations in 1977. The mediation efforts, spearheaded by the United States, were launched in April 1977 to obtain a settlement of the Namibian dispute along the lines set out in previous United Nations resolutions on Namibia, especially Security Council resolution 385 of 1976, which demanded, inter alia, that:

> South Africa accept elections under United Nations supervision and control before independence; (b) release of all political prisoners; (c) abolish all forms of racial discrimination; (d) permit all exiles to return without fear of arrest; and (e) withdraw its illegal administration.[104]

The Western nations further agreed that every stage and planning of this mediation effort would involve close consultation with the front line states and Nigeria. Since one of the objectives was a solution acceptable to all parties to the dispute, SWAPO was brought directly into the negotiating process. This was the beginning of the Contact Group, which included Canada, France, United Kingdom, United States and West Germany, and was headed by U.S. Ambassador Don McHenry.

Prompted by events in Angola in 1975 and pressures from the international community, South Africa realized that independence for Namibia was inevitable. However, South Africa's position as to what form it would take differed significantly from that of United Nations and SWAPO. Although South Africa did not wish to be seen as the one to break off negotiations with the Contact Group, it was unwilling to accept any solution that would jeopardize what it considered "to be vital political, strategic and economic interests in the territory."[105] From South Africa's point of view, the ideal solution was a friendly and dependent government in Namibia that would allow Namibia to remain a buffer state and permit continued South African access to the mineral wealth of the territory. And since the solution proposed by the Contact Group was perceived by South Africa as not likely to lead to a puppet government in Namibia that would allow South Africa to retain control of the territory's uranium and diamonds, South Africa presented its own alternative.

The Turnhalle Constitutional Talks

The talks, launched in September 1975 with representatives of the major ethnic groups, excluded SWAPO. In 1977 the conference produced a set of proposals for the establishment of an interim assembly that would lead to Namibian independence by December 1978.[106] The delegates from this conference, under South Africa's urgings, formed a multi-racial alliance party known as the Democratic Turnhalle Alliance (DTA), led by Dirk Mudge, a prosperous farmer of German extraction, who was reported to have a long history as a leader of a white supremacist party. South African sponsored elections that excluded SWAPO and other opposition parties was held on December 4–8, 1978 with predictable results. The DTA won in a landslide amidst worldwide condemnation of the entire exercise. The Contact Group branded the election outcome "null and void." SWAPO's secretary for foreign affairs Festus Naholo called "on all our brothers in Africa and the whole international community to condemn" the exercise.[107]

Observers saw the move as another unilateral declaration of independence and likened the December election in Namibia to Ian Smith's internal settlement. Xtopher Hitchens declared that:

> What we are seeing in Namibia is another Unilateral Declaration of Independence, only this time backed even more strongly by Pretoria because those involved are of South African, rather than British stock, and because the economic stake is more direct.[108]

With the lessons of Zimbabwe fresh in the minds of policymakers in South Africa, it seemed conceivable that South Africa's strategy was to: (a) eventually agree to an internationally-supervised election, (b) attempt to use the time gained by its delaying tactic to build up internal and external support of the DTA or (internal settlement), and (c) weaken SWAPO politically and militarily, thus, reduce its chances of winning the election when eventually held.

South Africa's attempt to side-track the international initiative may have slowed down the initial momentum gained when it appeared all parties to the conflict were willing to give the western plan a chance, but the plan was not discarded. The United Nations Council for Namibia held a series of extraordinary plenary meetings in Lusaka, Zambia in 1978. On March 23, 1978 it adopted a Declaration of Lusaka (A/S=9/2-S/12631) in which the Council said it considered the "illegal occupation of Namibia by South Africa to be a threat to international security." The Council recommended, among other things, that the General Assembly:

> . . . (a) urge the Security Council to take the necessary measures to end forthwith South Africa's illegal occupation of the territory; (b) ensure complete and unconditional withdrawal of South Africa from Namibia; and (c) urgently to consider the imposition of mandatory and comprehensive economic sanctions.[109]

On July 27, 1978 the Security Council endorsed the western initiative and adopted two Resolutions—431, on the appointment of a United Nations Commissioner for Namibia by a vote of 13 to 0; and 432, concerning Walvis Bay, by a unanimous vote. South Africa had attempted to a separate Walvis Bay from the rest of Namibia for possible annexation.

In Security Council Resolution 435, co-sponsored by Nigeria, the United States and others, the Council reiterated its major objective—the withdrawal of South Africa's illegal occupation of Namibia and the "transfer of power to the people of Namibia." Furthermore, the resolution:

> . . . (a) called for the establishment of the United Nations Transition assistance Group (UNTAG) to supervise the Namibian election; (b) called on South Africa forthwith to cooperate with the Secretary General in the implementation of its resolution, and with the UNTAG in carrying out its function; and (c) declared that all unilateral measure taken by the illegal administration in Namibia in relation to the electoral process, including unilateral registration of voters, or transfer of power, in contravention of Council resolutions 385, 431, and 435 were null and void.[110]

The resolution was adopted by a vote of 12 to 0, with two abstentions. The United Nations appointed Martti Ahtisaari as United Nations Commissioner for Namibia to head a negotiating team to work out the details of the cease fire and elections as stipulated by resolution 435.

Nigeria's Role

Nigeria not only endorsed the western initiative in Namibia, but threw its weight fully behind their efforts in 1977. Nigeria had consistently made its position on the Namibian question clear in both United Nations sessions and policy statement. In a speech delivered at the United Nations in 1977, Obsanjo reiterated Nigeria's commitment "to the cause of freedom and justice" in Namibia and added that" We salute SWAPO leaders and pay warm tributes to the devotion and determination of that organization to free Namibia from illegal occupation. We in Nigeria will not relent in our efforts to see Namibia free.[111] Nigeria's foreign affairs commissioner, Joe Garba, in a policy statement on October 21, 1977, not only reaffirmed Nigeria's position on Namibian, but deplored the 'hypocritical attitude on the part of some world powers in handling the Namibian question," and stated that "no sacrifice is too great, no measure too strong" for Nigeria to take to accelerate the process of decolonization and bring about genuine political change in Namibia.[112]

Shagari Administration

Shehu Shagari was elected President in 1979. His administration continued the activist foreign policy started by the Muhammed-Obasanjo regime. Shagari repeatedly reaffirmed Nigeria's commitment to the liberation of Namibia. Addressing the Lagos Diplomatic Corps, shortly after his inauguration, in 1979 Shagari said, "my administration will relentlessly work with all countries willing to apply civilized standards to bring about the early eradication of colonialism, racism and other forms of discrimination in Africa."[113]

On Namibia, Shagari reaffirmed "Nigeria's support for SWAPO as the sole and authentic representative of the people of Namibia." Declaring Nigeria's support for the Western initiative, Shagari urged the United Nations Secretary General to, "persist in his commendable efforts to implement the Security Council resolutions on Namibia. South Africa must withdraw unconditionally from that territory.[114] During his visit to the United States in 1980, Shagari predicted victory for Namibia in a year and called for mandatory sanctions against South Africa.

Efforts to find an internationally acceptable solution to the Namibian question continued during 1980, President Carter's last year in office. While the Untied Nations played a central role, it also received some assistance from Nigeria and the United States in keeping the issue alive.

Pre-implementation Conference (PIM)

During the Carter administration, South Africa moved grudgingly from intransigence to ambivalence to rather doubtful cooperation. By December

1980 South Africa was ready to come to the conference table.[115] In one of a series of attempts to resolve the Namibian dispute the United Nations sponsored a Pre-Implementation Conference (PIM) in Geneva in January 1981. Delegates to the meeting included the South African government and SWAPO, Nigeria, the frontline states, the AU and the Contract Group attended as observers. Specifically, this conference was called by the then United Nations Secretary General, Kurt Waldheim, for the purpose of setting the dates for a ceasefire; and the start of the implementation of the Settlement Proposal leading to independence for the territory in 1981.[116] The conference, opened by the Secretary General on January 7, ended on January 14 without agreement being reached on any of the two key points. Predictably, South Africa found another snag—this time expressing extreme concern "regarding the impartiality of the United Nations." In effect, South Africa was demanding the withdrawal of United Nations recognition of SWAPO as "the sole and authentic representative of the Namibian people."[117]

United Nations Under Secretary General for Special Political Affairs Brian E. Urquhart expressed regret at the failure of the conference, pointing out that by this failure "a great opportunity had been missed." Kurt Waldheim, in his report to the Security Council on the result of the conference dated January 19, 1981 stated that the outcome of the meeting "must give rise to the most serious international concern," and appealed to South Africa to reconsider its position.[118] At a United Nations press briefing on January 21, 1981, SWAPO's Permanent Observer to the United Nations, Theo-Ben Gurirab accused South Africa of wrecking the talks, and thus, forced the Namibian people on a war path. The General Assembly condemned "South Africa's maneuvers at the Geneva conference," and deplored the failure of the conference, which in the opinion of the Assembly, was attributable "to South Africa's continued intransigence." Furthermore, the Assembly expressed the view that, with failure of the Geneva talks, "the people of Namibia had no option other than to escalate their armed struggle."[119]

While South Africa continued to question the good faith of the United Nations in an apparent attempt to stall for time, it also stepped up building local support for its internal settlement, and actively pursued military action against SWAPO.

Ronald Reagan Elected

Observers noted that while the success of Mugabe in Zimbabwe served as a warning to South Africa over the future of Namibia, Ronald Reagan's election as United States President raised South Africa's hopes of a possible reversal of American support for an internationally acceptable settlement in

Namibia along the lines stipulated in Resolution 435. "The South African government," wrote the *Economist*, appears:

> . . . to be stalling yet again on the Namibia settlement plans. This time, it seems, Mr. Piet Botha's government wants another delay because it hopes it will be able to bargain for a better deal once the Reagan administration is in office in Washington. South Africa has long been banking on a Reagan administration coming to power and, it hoped, being both more sympathetic to is standpoint and more ready to veto a sanctions move.[120]

With the election of Ronald Reagan, reversal of American policy soon emerged, and there was a decided shift in perspective. This shift was anticipated by African observers when it became clear Reagan would be in the White House in 1981. Ali A. Mazrui, anticipating this shift, predicted that the Reagan administration was likely to have "an African policy that look at African issues neither on their merits nor from the perspective of direct U.S.–African relations, but from the perspective of U.S.–Soviet relations."[121] Richard Deutsch predicted that: (a) African concerns, such as the issue of political change in Africa, are not expected to be high priority issues in the Reagan administration, but added that pragmatism will lead the administration to accommodate "Nigeria's commitment to the achievement of majority rule" in southern Africa; and (b) the administration would back off from applying pressure on South Africa; instead it would engage the South African government in "frank talk" or "private persuasion."[122] Some of these predictions were right.

Constructive Engagement

Reagan's new approach was essentially coaxing rather than threatening South Africa into cooperation. The administration named this approach "constructive engagement." The corollary to this was the so-called "linkage"- which was a formula designed by the Reagan administration to make Namibia's independence contingent upon withdrawal of Cuban troops in Angola.[123] Critics charged that this policy hindered negotiations rather than helped them, pointing out that South Africa's refusal to withdraw from Namibia "for security reasons until 19,000 Cuban troops" are withdrawn from Angola, was in line with Reagan's policy of linkage. In Kenneth Kaunda's own words, "we cannot accept that. We do not see why there should be any connection between the withdrawals of the Cubans and independence for Namibia."[124] United States negotiators, headed by Assistant Secretary of State, Chester Crocker, explained the administration's position at home and abroad. He toured Africa in 1981 to explain United States policy on Africa, particularly in regard to Namibia. In a speech to United States Council on Foreign Relations in New York on October 5, 1981, Crocker branded the so-called United States tilt to South Africa as "misinformation," and added:

> We are determined to press for an internationally acceptable settlement for the independence of Namibia. That settlement must be one which meets the vital security needs of Namibia's neighbors as well as permits the exercise of self-determination by Namibia's people. We believe we have made progress toward that objective.[125]

Addressing the issue of linkage Crocker denied the existence of such a policy when he said: "We have not made Cuban troops withdrawal a pre-condition of the Namibian settlement. The Namibian negotiations are proceeding on their own track. However, Crocker echoed the administration's concern over the presence of Cuban troops which he saw as: "a major impediment to progress on Namibia, and a situation which allows the 'Soviet Union' and Cuba to foment disorder, to keep the pot boiling.[126]

Crocker's denials and explanations notwithstanding, Reagan made the independence of Namibia contingent upon the withdrawal of Cuban troops. Nigeria publicly rejected this, calling it "unjust" and "incomprehensible."

By the end of 1981 negotiations were at a standstill and announced deadlines passed with no solution insight. Even the unity of the Contact Group seemed to have unraveled, with France, Germany and Canada conceding that the only obstacle to an agreement was the Cuban issue, and informing Washington that linkage was unacceptable.

The question in Namibia was not political change per se, but what form it would take. Indications were that South Africa wanted to impose a neo-colonial form of government on Namibia in a desperate attempt to protect what it considered to be vital political, strategic and economic interests in the territory, and the Reagan administration seemed to be unwilling to discourage this. It is perhaps noteworthy that all the attendant problems that confronted Ian Smith's Internal Settlement were also present in the Namibian situation in that: (a) the war continued, (b) it attracted worldwide condemnation, and (c) South Africa's illegal occupation had not received international recognition. And it was clear that what happened to Ian Smith's Internal Settlement would also occur in Namibia. South Africa's delay tactics notwithstanding, colonial history repeated itself in Namibia.

The Brazzaville Protocol

After several more rounds of tripartite meetings in Brazzaville, Republic of the Congo, an agreement was finally reached on December 13, 1988.[127] A few days later, the agreement was signed by Angola, Cuba, and South Africa in a ceremony at the United Nations Headquarters in New York, chaired by the then United Nations Secretary-General Javier Perez de Cuelar and United States Secretary of State George P. Shultz on December 22, 1988, thus, ushering in the independence of Namibia on March 21, 1990. In spite of U.S. efforts to link Namibian independence to the removal of Russian and Cuban troops from Angola, which delayed the decolonization process, the outcome was predictable; all parties got most of what they wanted from the agreement. The United States achieved its stated objective: removal of Russian and Cuban troops, reasserted its influence in the region, stared down the Russians, and Nigeria, the United Nations the Contact Group, the Frontline states and Namibia also achieved their goal of independence. The mission for Angola, Cuba, and Russia was also accomplished.

Cooperation

The Reagan administration made meaningful cooperation between Nigeria and the United States on the Namibian question difficult because of its major policy shift.

First, both countries were not agreed on what the issue was in Namibia. Second, the Reagan administration intensified U.S. concern over Russia and Cuban involvement in Southern Africa, and U.S. access to strategic minerals and protection of its economic interests were the top priority issues for U.S. policy-makers, not African concerns and interests.

Nigeria's Motivations

Nigeria was motivated by the need to push the decolonization process one step further. As Africa's spokesman, with considerable involvement in the Southern African decolonization process, this became a natural issue over which all Nigerian administrations were agreed. Furthermore, it became an article of faith for all administrations in Nigeria to not only actively support the liberation of Southern Africa, but to regard it as a priority issue in its foreign policy.

United States' Motivations

While Nigeria saw colonialism as the problem in Namibia, the United States saw the Russian and the Cubans as the problem. Thus, for the Reagan administration, Namibia's independence took second place to the East-West confrontation. A SWAPO government in Namibia was seen by the Reagan administration as: (a) a victory for Russia and Cuba, (b) a blow to U.S. security, and (c) a loss of access to important strategic minerals.

Strategic Minerals

Namibia possesses extensive deposits of minerals including, uranium, diamonds, copper, lead and zinc. In 1977 Namibia was the seventeenth leading mining nation in the world, "with diamonds accounting for 66 percent of total mineral exports."[128]

Lithium and vanadium were produced extensively in Namibia and exported to the United States. Lithium is used in the manufacture of lubricants and ceramics, and vanadium is vital to the production of anti-corrosive steels. Furthermore, in 1977 Namibia was reported to be the second largest producer of lead in Africa, and "the third largest producer of Zinc." It is also rich in arsenic, silver, illuminate, salt, sodalities, gold, manganese, tin and slate.[129] In 1975 United States direct investment in Namibia was over $50 million.[130]

United States-owned Tsumeb Corporation and the Consolidated Diamond Mines of South West Africa, a member of the Anglo American Group produced "over 90 percent of all mineral production in Namibia."[131] It was estimated that Tsumeb's share of profit alone in 1978 amounted to $60 million.[132]

East-West confrontation and the protection of these varied economic and strategic interests took precedence over Namibian independence. In spite of these, the United States involvement in the negotiations was critical to the successful outcome in Namibia. After Namibia's independence the focus turned to South Africa itself. Efforts made by Nigeria and the United States to bring about political change in that country will be examined, and the motivations behind both countries' involvement will be highlighted in the following section.

SOUTH AFRICA

South Africa's apartheid system was unique, and of great concern to those committed to racial justice and human dignity. The question of how to transform South Africa's apartheid system bothered the rest of Africa for years. The concern shown by the rest of Africa for the achievement of this objective fluctuated throughout history. It was very intense immediately after periods of relative success of a liberation struggle or negotiated settlement in other parts of the continent.

Nigeria and the United States persistently expressed their opposition to South Africa's apartheid system. Both countries also made some efforts to bring about peaceful change in the apartheid system. The focus in this section is to: (a) identify the problem that existed in South Africa, (b) examine the positions taken by Nigeria and United States on the South African problem, and c) evaluate the roles both countries played in bringing about political change in South Africa, with some insights on the motivations behind both countries' involvement in South Africa.

Some highlights of the historical background of South Africa's apartheid system may be useful. The process of white dominance over the indigenous peoples of South Africa was set in motion in 1652 when the Dutch East India Company established the first permanent European settlement at the Cape of Good Hope.[133] This settlement facilitated the subsequent conquering of the territory. White domination over the African indigenous people was accomplished in three phases. First, whites occupied the arable land within 100 miles of Cape Town. By the 1800 they also controlled the fertile land throughout the whole of western half of the region. And by the end of the nineteenth century whites took complete control of the whole territory.[134]

By 1657 the settlement had grown into a colony, with the company releasing a number of its servants to become free settlers in the Cape in order to cultivate land and herd cattle. The Dutch settlers in the Cape quickly came to consider manual labor below their dignity; therefore, the company had to import slaves. The first shipload of slaves arrived in 1658.[135] Furthermore, the Dutch raided the local inhabitants for slaves, and with the increase in the number of Dutch settlers, came a sharp increase in the settlers' demand for cattle and land. African resistance to Dutch expansion was met with brute force, and by 1785 three additional settlements had been established by the Dutch: Stellenbosch settlement in 1685, Swellendam in 1747, and Graaff-Reinet in 1785.[136]

By the 18th century there were about 15,000 white settlers in the territory. Tension between the different groups of settlers existed, but their common Calvinist religion molded the white settlers into a relatively homogeneous group that became known as the Afrikaners. However, in about a generation, color had become "the primary index of status." Fundamentalist Afrikaners sought Biblical justification for racial segregation and white supremacy by arguing that, "Africans are the descendants of Ham, who was cursed by Noah, and are destined by God to be servants of servants, hewers of wood and drawers of water."[137]

British conquering of the territory in 1806 further complicated the South African situation. British-Afrikaner struggle for supremacy had sometimes overshadowed the traditional black-white power struggle. The result was what has become known as the Great Trek, in which Afrikaners, dissatisfied with British rule and its reforms which put the Africans on the same footing as the Afrikaner, traveled far into the interior, eventually establishing settlements in upper Natal.

Intra-white conflict notwithstanding, by the time South Africa became "independent" in 1910 whites were clearly in control. However, Africans had not been silent while whites took over control and designed the structure of South Africa's political system. African opposition was strong and organized. On the eve of South Africa's "independence," the National Native Convention protested the exclusion of Africans from political participation. That was the beginning of a movement that eventually gave rise to the formation of the African National Congress (ANC) in 1912. And until it was banned in 1960 following the Sharpeville massacre, "the ANC remained the chief standard-bearer" and a major force in the liberation struggle in South Africa.[138]

The Problem

The uniqueness of South Africa's apartheid system, in the words of a United States Senator, was that "its policies are based on race, made legal through legislation, and justified in the name of defending the West from Communism."[139] The racially dominated state was controlled by and existed for the purpose of upholding the privileges of a white minority. These privileges included, among other things: (a) the consumption of 60 percent of the nation's income, (b) ownership of 87 percent of the land, and (c) control of "most of the skilled and semi-skilled occupations."[140]

Apartheid provided the guiding principle for government action and legislation. What followed particularly from 1948 was a systematic barrage of laws and regulations which imposed requirements for separate facilities, separate group areas, and racial classifications; prohibited sexual relations between different races and practically prohibited any form of meaningful interaction between the races in all aspects of life.[141] To implement and enforce such a vast apparatus of laws and regulations, the South African regime had to create a substantial bureaucracy. A person's fundamental rights hinged on the color of his or her skin. Thus, the South African regime divided the population into four groups: Africans, Asians, Coloreds, and whites. The legal basis of this division stemmed from the Population Registration Act of 1950. Under this law, sometimes described as the cornerstone of apartheid, the government can further reclassify people. The implication here was that in South Africa one could be classified as a member of more than one racial group at different times. According to a United States Commission report:

> In 1978 ten whites were reclassified as colored and 150 colored were reclassified as white. Such shifts can cause upheavals in families. Families are torn

apart when husbands, wives, parents and children, brothers and sisters are differently classified, with all the ensuing consequences to their personal, economic and political lives.[142]

To guard against racial crossings the South African regime enacted legal prohibitions against mixed marriages and interracial dating. In 1959 the Prohibition of Mixed Marriages Act was passed. It forbids marriages between a European and a non-European. Other laws in the same general category included the Immorality Acts of 1957 and 1950 which outlawed sexual relations or "any immoral or indecent act" between blacks and whites. About six hundred people were convicted in 1960; and 355 people were charged under the Immorality Acts in 1980 alone.[143]

The "Homelands"

The homelands policy, developed in the 1950s effectively revoked the citizenship of the African majority. They would become citizens of the independent homelands, who would only work in South Africa as foreign guest workers with temporarily work permits. This policy reached its climax in 1976 with the granting of "independence" to Transkei. One of the bases of this policy was the Promotion of Bantu Self-Government Act of 1959 which implied that Africans would never be permitted effective participation in South Africa except in their designated tribal homelands. In other words, this policy was designed to ensure that whites retained control of 87 percent of the territory while the African majority were restricted to these tribal states. Thus, whites would not have to share political and economic power with Africans, but would retain African labor. The Report of the Study Commission summed up the ultimate goal of this policy as follows:

> All homelands should become independent states: the entire African population of the Republic would be granted political rights and citizenship in these states; consequently, there would ultimately be no African citizen of the Republic of South Africa requiring accommodation in the political order of South Africa itself.[144]

Some of the most detested aspects of apartheid were the pass laws. The Black Urban Areas Consolidation Act of 1945 and the Black Abolition of Passes and Coordination of Document Act of 1952 were the main statutes restricting the entry of Africans into white areas. The pass laws in effect required that:

> Africans must carry at all times a reference book containing his employment history, as well as a number of documents; such as tax receipts. . . . Africans may

not reside anywhere without permission, may not move outside his allotted place of residence without approval of the authorities, is subject to curfew at night, may not live in any 'white' area without being gainfully employed, may not own land in freehold, and may be expelled form his residence and deported to any place, when the administration deems his presence to be 'undesirable.'[145]

Compounding these discriminatory laws was the total exclusion of blacks from effective political participation.

Furthermore, blacks were struggling not only against, "the all-embracing" exploitations they had been subjected to in the apartheid system, they were challenging, "a history of violation that goes far beyond the judicial, into that which is economic and social as well."[146]

Education

There were serious inequalities in the education of blacks as compared to that of whites in South Africa. These inequalities ranged from physical facilities to textbooks. In 1979 the teacher-pupil ratio was: (a) 1 to 48 for blacks, and 1 to 30 for Colored, compared with 1 to 20 for whites. Dropouts' rates in black schools were very high. In 1967 the attrition rate was about 80 percent. In 1970 there were only 1,400 blacks with university education, while there were 104,500 whites with university education.[147]

The gross injustice of apartheid as it related to education can be best gleaned from government expenditures on white and black education. In the fiscal year 1978–1979, the apartheid regime spent $90 on each black child, $290 on each Colored child, and $940 on each white child. Thus, in 1981 40 percent of the urban black workforce was classified as functionally illiterate, in the rural areas, the figure was 65 percent.[148]

There was a wide gap between white and black wages for equal work. Specifically, it was 5 to 1 in 1981. In the same year it was estimated that African per capital income was $280, compared to white per capital income of $3,5000. About 85 percent of blacks worked for the minimum wage, compared with 0.24 percent of whites.[149] Correcting these inequalities and other aspects of apartheid was the early focus of the struggle.

Focus of the Struggle

It was abundantly clear the struggle in South Africa involved a dangerous confrontation between a minority white population, pursuing discriminatory policies designed to keep them in control of the state they captured over a half century ago, and the majority of oppressed, exploited and dispossessed Africans determined to wrest political power from the apartheid regime and institute in its place a system based on majority rule, one man one vote.

The struggle to wrest political power from the repressive apartheid regime gave rise to a number of liberation movements in South Africa. The major one was the African National Congress (ANC). Others included the Black Consciousness Movement (BCM) and the Pan-Africanist Congress (PAC), (a splinter group from the ANC). At its peak the ANC claimed a membership of approximately 100,000 committed to the liberation of South Africa. Before the ANC was driven underground in 1960 under the terms of the Suppression of Communism Act, it led the fight inside South Africa against the Native Land Act of 1913. Under this law the white minority took 87 percent of the land , and left 13 percent for the African majority. The ANC supported the bloodily repressed Sharpeville protest of 1960 and the students uprising of 1976 in Soweto, both viewed as turning points in black militancy. The ANC was a viable organization with a well-established network of internal and external supporters and sources of money. Studies show that the ANC enjoyed widespread support among South African blacks. About 55 percent of the people polled in Soweto in 1978 expressed support for ANC, and the number jumped to 69 per cent in 1980.[150] Cuba, Nigeria, the Front Line States and Russia were some of the major backers of the ANC. The ANC also received financial and moral support from the British Labor Party and the World Council of Churches.

Nigeria and United States Positions

Opposition to the apartheid system not only came from internal groups but also from external forces. The opposition of Nigeria and the United States to the apartheid system was reiterated by both countries on several occasions.

Nigeria

Radical Pan-Africanists stressed that the survival of the apartheid system rested on the fact that African countries capable of meeting South Africa's humiliating challenge did not step forward to do so. That assessment was debatable. However, beginning with the Muhammed-Obasanjo regime, Nigeria stepped forward to make its contribution toward meeting the humiliating challenge. Almost immediately after his ascendancy to power in 1975 Muhammad tried to provide leadership, particularly in matters concerning political change in South Africa. In a policy statement on September 1, 1975, the Nigerian Government strongly condemned the apartheid system and sought to ostracize South Africa from the international community; called on member states of the United Nations to avoid economic relations with South Africa and further tightening of United Nations arms embargo on South.

After less than a year in office, Muhammad was assassinated. His successor Olusegun Obasanjo took over in February 1976. Essentially, no reversal of policy was undertaken during his administration. Instead, Obsanjo favored a tough stance on apartheid by developing a comprehensive policy that placed equal weight on armed liberation and diplomatic initiatives. In an effort to prepare the general public for possible Nigerian military involvement in South Africa and raise national consciousness about the struggle in South Africa, the Nigerian Government undertook a massive publicity campaign to educate the people of Nigeria about the situation in South Africa. *The Southern Africa Relief Fund* was established in late 1976, and by mid 1977 more than $10 million was collected. The first of a number of airlifts of relief supplies that included shoes and blanket sent by the Fund to the liberation movement left Lagos on September 7, 1977.[151] Countries that had suffered from the effects of liberation war were also earmarked for special assistance to help offset economic losses caused by the war. In April 1976 Nigeria gave Mozambique a grant for $1.5 million, and in July another check for $250,000 for the support of Zimbabwe freedom fighters was handed to Joaquin Chissano, Mozambique's Minister of Foreign Affairs. In January 1977 another airlift of relief supplies left Lagos for Botswana for an estimated 2,000 South African refugees there. And in January 1977 alone 200 Soweto refugee students were admitted to schools and universities in Nigeria.[152]

It was against this background that the announcement in June 1977 by the Chief of Staff, Lt. Gen. T.Y. Danjuma that Nigeria was ready to send troops to assist the liberation movements particularly in South Africa was received favorably throughout the country.

Nigeria's efforts at peaceful change were also demonstrated through unilateral actions, diplomatic pressures exerted through international forums and joint diplomatic initiatives with the Untied States. In his position as Chairman of the United Nations Special Committee against Apartheid, Leslie Harriman, Nigeria's Ambassador to the Untied Nations consistently worked to put the issue of political change in South Africa on the front political burner. One of such efforts was the World Conference for Action Against Apartheid held in Lagos from August 22–26, 1977. The Conference was organized by the Nigerian Government in cooperation with the African Union, the U.N. and in consultation with the South African liberation movements, the ANC and the PAC. Participants were 112 Governments, including the frontline states, the Untied States and Britain, 12 inter-governmental organizations, five liberation movements and five non-governmental organizations.

The purpose of the conference was to intensify the international campaign against apartheid and map out, as Kurt Waldheim puts it, "a program of effective action commanding the widest possible support from the international community."[153] Leslie Harriman said at the conference that: "The time has come for the international community to pledge to stamp out apartheid, a refined form of slavery, as it abolished slavery a century ago."[154] Speaking before the conference, the Untied States Ambassador to the United Nations, Andrew Young, credited the Nigerian government with bringing about a new sensitivity of the West" to apartheid. He saw apartheid as "a policy of discrimination and racism that most Americans had known at home in not so distant a past." He likened the apartheid system to cancer, but one that can be cured without necessarily killing the patient.[155] Furthermore, he reiterated the Untied States commitment to bring about change in South Africa, leading to majority rule and an end to apartheid.

Also speaking before the conference Obasanjo stated that Nigeria was willing to move from rhetoric to concrete action. The conference adopted a 30-point Declaration that came to be known as the Lagos Declaration.[156]

Throughout 1977 the Obasanjo administration discussed ways of forcing western firms doing business in South Africa to choose between their interests in South Africa and in black Africa. By he end of 1977 Nigeria had established an Economic Intelligence Unit to prevent firms that had dealings with South Africa from operating in Nigeria. The first of a number of retaliatory measures was announced on March 21, 1978. Nigeria ordered the withdrawal of all government deposits from Barclays Bank.[157] This move almost caused the bank to fail. In December 1977, the United Nations General Assembly overwhelmingly endorsed a proposal for a mandatory oil embargo against South Africa, and Nigeria took the proposal to the Security Council in early 1978.

Obasanjo left office in 1979, and his successor, President Shehu Shagari repeatedly reaffirmed Nigeria's commitment to the end of apartheid. He vowed to continue the policy of taking a tough stance against "western business interests that continue to collaborate with South Africa." Furthermore, he warned that Nigeria would use "all means at our disposal, including oil if necessary," to bring about political change in South Africa.[158]

United States

On South Africa, the Untied States, especially during the Carter administration, seemed to favor a tough stance on apartheid. This tough stance was manifested in three forms of pressure: military, economic, and diplomatic.

Military

Historically, curbs on military cooperation with South Africa appeared to have been the most important on the list of United States action taken against apartheid. In 1963 United States embargoed arms sales to South Africa, and in 1967 the United States Navy was ordered to stop calling at South African ports. United States voted for Untied Nations Security Council Resolution 418 which imposed a mandatory arms embargo against South Africa in 1977. The embargo was adopted unanimously by the 15 members of the Security Council in a vote the Secretary General Kurt Waldheim called "a momentous step." Andrew Young later said that the arms embargo was not aimed at destroying the apartheid regime but was an attempt to encourage moderation in South Africa. In 1978 a ban was placed on export of items used by the South African military and police, deemed to be the chief enforcers of apartheid.

Economics

Although Andrew Young had argued that economic sanctions, whether partial or total, were never effective, limited economic pressure was applied on South Africa by the United States. In 1979 Congressional committee investigations revealed that Olin Corporation was involved in the illegal shipment of arms to South Africa. A total of 3,200 guns were reported illegally shipped between 1971 and 1975, for which the company was fined $510,000. Also, voters in Berkeley, California, voted overwhelmingly to withdraw city funds from United States banks that had extended loans to South Africa.[159] Furthermore, the export and import Bank was forbidden to: (a) make loans for United States sales to South Africa; and (b) extend guarantees or credit insurance to United States businesses operating in South Africa unless they could show evidence of progress being made in eliminating apartheid.[160] Also, United States and about 140 United States firms doing business in South Africa endorsed the Sullivan Principles.[161]

Diplomacy

Quiet diplomatic talks with South Africa on apartheid produced no tangible results. One such occasion was in 1977 when Vice President Mondale, at a meeting in Vienna, bluntly told B.J. Vorster that relations between United States and South Africa would depend on progress toward the elimination of apartheid. In a policy statement on June 20, 1978 Secretary of State, Cyrus Vance reiterated the Administration's tough stance when he said:

> We have made it clear to the South African government that a failure to begin to make genuine progress toward an end to racial discrimination and full political participation for all. . . . citizens can only have an increasingly adverse impact on our relations.[162]

By 1980 the Carter administration left no doubts in the minds of observers and the South African regime that a definite departure from the Nixon-Ford

administration policy had been established. The State Department group during the Carter administration that was partly responsible for this departure
was the Africanists, made up of secretary of State Cyrus Vance, U.S. Ambas-
sadors to the Untied Nations, Andre Young, and Don McHenry. The administration's policy closely followed the thinking of this group who, believed,
"that African problems should be dealt with as much as possible on their own
merits, and that apartheid is not only morally wrong but historically
doomed."[163]

The Reagan administration did not deal with African problems on their
own merits. Rather, it dealt with African problems within the context of the
East-West confrontation. President Reagan tended to be supportive of the
South African regime. Reagan defended United States support on "both moral
and strategic grounds." In 1981 President Reagan said:

> As long as there is a sincere and honest effort being made (by the apartheid
> regime), based on our own experience in our land, it would seem to me that we
> should be trying to be helpful. . . . Can we abandon a country . . . that strategi-
> cally is essential to the Free World in its production of minerals we all must have
> and so forth.[164]

It was in this context that five South African military officers visited the
United States in 1981. They were received by Jeane Kirkpatrick, United
States Ambassador to the United Nations. Observers pointed out that the
South Africans' visits and consultations with Untied States officials "violated
a long standing policy outlawing official business visits to this country by
members of South Africa's armed forces."[165]

The shift in United States policy under the Reagan administration undermined what little progress had been made by the Africanist Group in the
Carter administration to bring about change in the apartheid system.

Evaluation

The effect of these combined pressures from Nigeria and the Untied States
with collaboration from the Untied Nations, coupled with the escalation of
guerrilla activities inside South Africa produced two responses form South
Africa: (1) minimizing its dependence on foreign arms and oil; and (2) initiating some cosmetic changes that did very little to change the material conditions of the African majority in South Africa.

The South African regime attempted to counter the arms embargo by: (a)
stepping up the production of arms. In 1979 it was estimated that South Africa
had built the world's tenth largest arms industry, possibly including a nuclear
weapons capabilities and (b) once heavily dependent on foreign oil, South

Africa minimized that dependence to 22 percent of its oil needs in 1980. South Africa developed the largest and technologically the most advanced "oil-from-coal industry in the continent. The goal for South Africa was to be self-sufficient in energy in two decades.

The cosmetic changes initiated by South African regime included the relaxation of "petty apartheid," such as discrimination in cinemas, parks, sports and beaches. These changes were contained in three new laws announced by the South African regime towards the end of 1980. The new laws were aimed at eliminating hurtful discrimination. Perhaps the most important aspect of these laws concerned the attempt to deal with the presence of Africans in the so-called white areas outside the homelands. These laws repealed the Urban Areas Act and "change the pass law system and influx control regulation which restricted the flow of blacks to the cities."[166]

Supporters hailed these changes as "revolutionary breakthrough in race relations," and predicted the end to the pass law system. Critics rejected it as being too little too late because "it did not involve fundamental changes in the apartheid structure, and was merely an adjustment within the framework."[167] On the other hand, the ANC stepped up guerilla attacks inside South Africa. Two crucial Sasol oil-for-coal plants were set ablaze in 1980.

Earlier, students trade unions and several organizations were involved in activism inside South Africa. Students protests against being taught in Afrikaans led to the Soweto uprising of June 1976. Within a few weeks the uprising escalated into a large resistance movement. It triggered simultaneous uprisings by colored and Indian students, some sectors of black workers, and some white students marched in solidarity with Soweto.[168] The Soweto uprising "became a political act and a general declaration of war on the white rule."[169] In 1980 colored students in the Cape area went on a prolonged strike causing a violent confrontation with the South African police.

The formation of black and multi-racial trade unions was sanctioned in South Africa in 1979. That in itself was considered an achievement by South Africa standards because in theory, trade unions were forbidden to engage in political activities, but 1979 witnessed the fastest growth ever in militancy of the trade union movement. Although the unions claimed they were not political , that heir focus was solely on pay and conditions, observers pointed out that "the possibility of organized labor acting as a potent vehicle for political change" was obvious.[170]

The Federation of South African Trade Unions (FOSATU) followed a carefully planned strategy of fighting those battles which they had some chance of winning. Its general secretary Alec Erwin said the unions made some gains in relaxation of petty apartheid in workplaces, but he also pointed out that once outside the workplace, workers were still confronted with apartheid.

Reagan and Apartheid

Critics believed United States, particularly the Reagan administration, did not do enough to promote the cause of African emancipation. They demanded stronger actions, including a trade boycott, disinvestment and a mandatory application of the Sullivan Principles against the South African government. Randall Robinson, lamented the lack of serious commitment to change on the part of the United States, pointing out that:

> . . . . the difficulty is that Americans often do not identify with the struggle for change in South Africa. We lack a serious commitment to change, because as a nation we tend to identify with the plight of white South Africans.[171] A case against disinvestment as effective action against the apartheid regime was made by those who contended that disinvestment would hurt blacks.

Yet others wanted United States to apply stronger pressure on South Africa to bring about change of the Apartheid system; and complained that United States lacked the domestic political will to do so. A study done for the Carnegie Endowment for International peace concluded that: "there is a clear consensus in the foreign policy community that the Untied States should exert stronger pressure on the South African regime to change its domestic racial policies." The study added that beneath the consensus that fundamental change in South Africa was inevitable, and that United States should apply pressure on South Africa, "lie a host of contradictions, inconsistencies and disagreements."[172] Of critical significance was the disagreement about the degree of change that was needed in South Africa and how it would come about.

Fundamental change in the apartheid system, involving a major restructuring of government and society, was what was needed. That change came in the late 1980s.

Change in South Africa

In 1984 the South Africa government recognized the inevitability of change when South African President P.W. Botha told white South Africans to "adapt or die." But Botha stopped short of initiating fundamental change.

Negotiated Settlement

Success of the Liberation movement and international pressure forced South Africa to the negotiating table. P.W. Botha left office in 1989 and was replaced by F.W de Klerk, who held secret talks with ANC leaders and Nelson Mandela to prepare South Africans for his "unbanning" speech on Feb. 2 1990 in which he lifted the ban on ANC, UDF, the PAC and the Communist Party. Many political prisoners were released, including Nelson Mandela, who was released from prison Feb 11, 1990, after serving 27 years at the Victor Vester prison. A year later, South Africa was ready for negotiation for majority rule.

Convention for a Democratic South Africa

In 1991 negotiations started under the auspices of CODESA[173] and after months of wrangling and several rounds of negotiations, a compromise was reached and election date was set. In 1993 a draft constitution was published,[174] and elections were held on April 27, 1994. The ANC won 62.7% percent of the vote and Nelson Mandela became president with Thabo Mbeki and De Klerk as deputies. A new constitution was adopted in 1995, thus putting to rest the last vestiges of apartheid in South Africa.

What were the factors behind U.S. policy in South Africa? Diplomatic rhetoric aside, was the U.S. really committed to fundamental change in South Africa? Why did the U.S. drag its feet in applying stronger pressure on South Africa? Were Nigeria and the U.S. both motivated by the same interests in South Africa?

Motivations

There was evidence to suggest that both countries were not motivated by the same interests. While Nigeria was motivated by its sincere commitment to political change, the United States sought to protect its varied economic and strategic interests in South Africa.

Nigeria

The need to complete the unfinished task of the total decolonization of Southern Africa was a strong motivating factor for Nigeria's involvement in South Africa. Furthermore, Nigeria saw this task as a moral obligation on its part to assist fellow Africans in the liberation of what remains of the white redoubt. The liberation of South Africa was a fulfilling achievement for Nigeria which had consistently stressed the point that until all of Africa was free, Nigeria remains unfree.

United States

Beyond the level of diplomatic rhetoric, the United States was not interested in fundamental change in South Africa, particularly during the Reagan administration. The motivating factors behind U.S. policy in South Africa were essentially strategic and economic.

Strategic Interests

These included: (a) U.S. access to South Africa's mineral resources, (b) the security of Western oil flows around the Cape Sea route, and (c) containing Russian and Cuban influence and activities in South Africa. Platinum, a major element in anti-polution technology, was one of the many minerals imported by the United States from South Africa. Others included, antimony, (44%), manganese (9%), Cobalt (7%), and industrial diamonds (81%). (See Table 3.1). It was estimated that South Africa had about half of the world's gold resources, and produced about 60 percent of the total world's production. The Cape Sea route, connecting the South Atlantic and the Indian Oceans, serves as a passageway for 90 percent of Western Europe's oil supplies, 70 percent of its strategic minerals, and about 20 percent of U.S. oil imports.[175] The U.S. also had an interest in maintaining its naval base in Simonstown, South Africa, in order to continue its space tracking stations, activities and intelligence operations in the region and much of black Africa.

A prolonged cut-off of these supplies by Russia could cripple Western economies. Therefore, Russia's access to basing rights in South Africa would be considered by the U.S. as giving the Russians the military means to do so.

Economic Interests

The U.S corporate stake in South Africa included about 350 American companies, with a total investment of about $2 billion in 1980. (See Table 2). Rhetorical condemnation of apartheid notwithstanding, the U.S. government actually facilitated U.S. investments in South Africa. According to a study for the U.S. Department of Commerce, U.S. Embassy staff in South Africa "consider the rendering of assistance to present and potential U.S. investors to be a vital part of its task in the country," and indeed, this commanded a considerable portion of the embassy's attention."[176] Furthermore, the U.S. had lucrative trade relations with South Africa, totaling $3.4 billion in 1980.[177]

Nation states formulate their foreign policies to promote and defend their most vital interests. No doubt these strategic and economic interests in South Africa were vital national interests to the U.S., but so were the changing realities in southern Africa as were public opinion.

In the concluding chapter, an attempt will be made to: (a) sum up the impact of Nigeria-United States roles on these cases; (b) generalize about relations between Nigeria and the United States with respect to political change in Africa, with an update on relations between the two countries after decolonization and, (c) critically evaluate the prospects for Nigeria-United States relations in the future.

NOTES

1. Guinea Bissau and Mozambique won independence in 1973 and 1975, respectively. In both cases independence was won largely through armed struggle led by PAIGC in Guinea Bissau and FRELIMO in Mozambique.
2. Douglas Wheeler and R. Pelissier, *Angola* (New York: Praeger, 1971), 32.
3. *Africa*, n 52 (December 1975): 88.
4. Basil Davidson, *In the Eye of the Storm* (New York: Doubleday, 1972), 97.
5. Basil Davidson, *In the Eye of the Storm* p. xiii.
6. For a detailed discussion of the ideology used to explain and justify the Portuguese presence in Africa, see G.J. Bender, *Angola Under the Portuguese* (Los Angeles: UCLA Press, 1978).
7. G.J. Bender, *Angola Under the Portuguese* (Los Angeles: UCLA Press, 1978).
8. Henrique Galvao, *Report on Native Problems in the Portuguese Colonies* (Lisbon, 1970), 57–71.
9. Henrique Galvao, *Report on Native Problems*, 57–71.
10. Mario de Souza Clington, *Angola Libre?* (Paris: Gallimard, 1975) 133. This decree: (a) gave high priority to the settlement of Portuguese in Angola, (b) declared most of the land as the property of the state, and (c) forced 90 percent of the Africans off the land to make room for the settlement of thousands of Portuguese in rural Angola.
11. Bender, *Angola Under the Portuguese*, 149.
12. For a partial list of liberation movements in Angola, see John Marcum, *The Angolan Revolution* vol. 2 (Cambridge, Mass.: MIT Press, 1978), 318.
13. Irving Kaplan, *Angola: A Country Study* (Washington, D.C.: American University Press, 1979), 45.
14. Irving Kaplan, *Angola: A Country Study*; 45.
15. "United Nations Resolution 1819 (XVII)" *U.N. General Assembly Official Records* vol. 1, Seventeenth Session, 1962.
16. G. Giovanni, "Can Colonialism Make It?" Atlas vol. 9, n 6 (June 1965): 353–359.
17. Marcum, *The Angolan Revolution*, 241.
18. Marcum, *The Angolan Revolution*, 241.
19. For more details see Colin Legum, *Africa Contemporary Records*: 1975–1976 (New York: Africana publishing), 797(B).
20. For a discussion of guerilla movements in Angola see Marcum, *The Angolan Revolution*, 241.
21. Charles K. Ebinger, "External Intervention in Internal War: The Politics and Diplomacy of the Angolan Civil War," *Orbis*, Fall 1976, 671.
22. *Report of the 'OAU' Conciliation Commission's Recommendations on Angola*, adopted at the OAU Summit in Kampala, October 24, 1975.
23. "The Nature and Extent of the South African Defense Forces Involvement in the Angolan Conflict," Defense Headquarters Communiqué, Pretoria, February 3, 1977.
24. National Security Of Council Inter-Dept. Group for Africa, *Study in Response to NSSM 39: Southern Africa, AF-NSE-1969*, August 15, 1969.

25. See also Henry F. Jackson, *From the Congo to Soweto: U.S. Foreign Policy Toward Africa Since 1960* (New York: W. Morrow & Co., 1982).

26. *Department of State Bulletin*, August 11, 1975, 212.

27. Legum, *Africa Contemporary Records*: 1974–75, 97–99 (A).

28. Secretary of States Henry A. Kissinger, *Implications of Angola for Future U.S. Foreign Policy*, Testimony made before the Senate Committee on Foreign Relations on January 29, 1976, Washington, D.C.

29. John Marcum, "Lessons of Angola," *Foreign Affairs*, April 1976, 414.

30. John Stockwell, *In search of Enemies: A CIA Story* (New York: W.W. Norton Press, 1978) 54.

31. *Congressional Quarterly*, December 20, 1975, 2832.

32. Stockwell, *In Search of Enemies*, 54.

33. Edward A. Hawley et al., "Angolan Independence: Agony and Hope," *Africa Today* (October 1975): 7.

34. *Congressional Quarterly*, 27 December 1975, 2854.

35. *Congressional Quarterly*, 31 December 1976, 208.

36. Kissinger, *Implications of Angola*, 5.

37. "President Ford Reiterates U.S. Objective in Angola, *Department of State Bulletin*, 16 February 1976, 182–183.

38. Marcum, "Lessons of Angola," 419.

39. Kissinger, *Implications of Angola*, 7.

40. Marcum, *The Angolan Revolution*, 235.

41. Jackson, *From Congo to Soweto*, 59.

42. For a detailed discussion of the political history of Zimbabwe, see Philip Mason, *The Birth of a Dilemma* (New York: Preager, 1958).

43. The most useful is given by Patrick O' Meara, in *Rhodesia: The Racial Conflict or Coexistence?* (New York: Cornell University Press, 1975).

44. Irving Kaplan, *Rhodesia: A Country Study* (Washington, D.C.: American University Press, 1979) xii.

45. Leonard T. Kapungu, *Rhodesia: The Struggle for Freedom* (New York: *Orbis Books*, 1974) 14.

46. Leonard T. Kapungu, *Rhodesia: The Struggle*, 19.

47. Harold D. Nelson et al., *Area Hand Book for Southern Rhodesia* (Washington, D.C.: American).

48. Patrick O' mear, "Rhodesia-Zimbabwe: Guerilla Warfare or Political Settlement?" in *Southern Africa: The Continuing Crisis*, Gwendolen M. Carter and Patrick O'Meara, eds. (Bloomington: Indiana University Press, 1979) 19.

49. O'Meara, "Rhodesia-Zimbabwe," 24.

50. ZAPU and ZANU merged on October 10, 1976 to form the Patriotic Front.

51. *Africa Contemporary Records* 1976–77, 19(A).

52. *The Daily Telegraph*, 26 January 1979, 5.

53. David Martin and Phyllis Johnson, *The Struggle for Zimbabwe* (New York: Monthly Review Press, 1981), 280.

54. *Africa Contemporary Records* 1976–77, 911–12(B).

55. *Lusaka Manifesto on Southern Africa*: Joint Statement by the OAU Assembly of Heads of State and Government held in Lusaka, Zambia on April 16, 1969.

56. *Lusaka Manifesto on Southern Africa*, 2.

57. *Lusaka Manifesto on Southern Africa*, 2.

58. *Department of State Bulletin*, 31 May 1976, 672.

59. *New Proposals for a Settlement: British Government White Paper* (London: 1 September 1977).

60. This document formed the basis for the Lancaster House Agreement of 1979.

61. *Nigeria Bulletin on Foreign Affairs*, vol. 7, no. 9 (September 1977): 4.

62. *Nigeria Bulletin on Foreign Affairs*, 4.

63. For example, the specially-entrenched provisions of the constitution could be amended only with the affirmative votes of 78 members of the House of Assembly. This requirement of more than three-quarter votes effectively gave whites a veto power over any proposed amendment. For further details see Documents Section, *Africa Contemporary Records*, 1977–78, 5 (C). Martin and Johnson, *The Struggle for Zimbabwe*, 293.

64. Patriotic Front's Leader R. Mugabe, quoted by Anthony Lewis, *New York Times*, 7 February 1979, 10(A).

65. *The Guardian*, 1 December 1978, 5.

66. United Nations Security Council Resolution 423.

67. *Time*, 30 April 1979, 36.

68. For an overview, see T. Mutunhu, "Internal Settlement: A Sell-Out," *Black Scholar* (September 1978): 2.

69. Reports by observers indicate the elections were neither free nor fair. For full details of reports, see Claire Palley, *The Rhodesian Election* (London: Catholic Institute for International Relations, April 1979), (mimeographed).

70. *Africa Contemporary Records*, 1978–79, 975(B).

71. *Time*, April 1979, 36.

72. *The Herald* (Salisbury), 14 February 1979, 1.

73. *Economist*, 7 July 1979, 78.

74. The *Daily Times*, 5 July 1979, 2.

75. "Carter Rhodesia Policy Suffer a Set Back in Senate," *Congressional Quarterly* (19 May 1979): 957.

76. *New Nigerian*, 6 June 1979, 3.

77. *Washington Post*, 12 December 1979, 5 (A).

78. *Economist*, 26 May 1979, 13.

79. *The Daily Telegraph*, 14 June 1979, 10.

80. *West Africa*, 6 August 1979, 1399.

81. Quoted by Martyn Gregory, in Rhodesia: "From Lusaka to Lancaster House," *The World Today* (January 1980): 13.

82. Other trouble spots, including Namibia and South Africa itself, and the growing African refugee problem were discussed.

83. *Final Communiqué of the Meeting of Commonwealth Heads of Government*, held in Lusaka, Zambia, 1–7 August 1979 (Commonwealth Secretariat, London).

84. While Kenneth Kaunda, Chairman of the conference, was jubilant, the Muzorewa regime was angry because Thatcher had changed her position, and the Patriot Front expressed skepticism.

85. Martyn Gregory, "Rhodesia: From Lusaka," 17.

86. By the end of 1980 the U.S. had made a $50 million donation to that fund.

87. Martyn Gregory, "The 1980 Rhodesian Elections: A First Hand Account and Analysis," *The World Today* (May 1980): 180.

88. "Britain Rules Rhodesia After Truce," *Africa Report* (January–February 1980): 23.

89. ZANU won 63 percent of the popular vote and 57 of 80 black Assembly seats.

90. It is perhaps of some historical significance to note that President Carter's visit in April 1978 was the only state visit to a sub-Saharan African country ever made by a U.S. president.

91. Harold D. Nelson, ed. *Nigeria: A Country Study* (Washington, D.C.: American University Press, 1982) 231.

92. *U.S. Military Involvement in Southern Africa*, (ed) ACAS (Boston: South End Press, 1978) 25.

93. Ann and Neva Seidman, *South Africa and U.S. Multinational Corporation* (Westport, Conn.: Lawrence Hill, 1977), 213.

94. For a review, see Christopher Hitchens, "Namibia-Rhodesia Again?" *Nation*, 30 December 1978, 725.

95. President Wilson is credited as being the main champion of the planning and writing processes of the League of Nations.

96. "What is Namibia? Some Highlights of Territory's History," *United Nations Chronicle XVIII*, no. 6 (June 1981): 13.

97. *United Nations Chronicle*, June 1981, 13.

98. *United Nations General Assembly Official Records*, Sixteenth Session, 1960–61, 158.

99. *South West Africa, Second Phase, Judgment: I.C. J. Reports*, 1966, 6.

100. United Nations Resolution 2145 9XXI, *U.N. Resolutions Series* 1, vol. XI, 1966–68, 118.

101. Among those in contention for power are the South West African National United Front (SWANUF) the South West African National Union (SWANU) and the South West African Peoples Organization (SWAPO).

102. *Declaration of the Central Committee of the SWAPO*, by Sam Nujoma in Lusaka, Zambia, 2 August 1976.

103. Secretary of State Henry Kissinger, *U.S. Policy on Southern Africa*, an Address made on April 25, 1976 at Lusaka, Zambia. Also see *Department of State Bulletin* 31 May 1976, 672–684.

104. *United Nations Chronicle*, XII, no. 2 (February 1976): 18.

105. Michael Spicer, "Namibia: Elusive Independence," *World Today*, October 1980, 407.

106. Spicer, "Namibia: Exclusive Independence," 409.

107. *Washington Post*, 20 August 1976, 7(A).

108. Xopher Hitchens, "Namibia: Rhodesia Again," *Nation*, 30 December 1978, 726.

109. *Annual Review of United Nations Affairs*, 1978, 61.

110. *Annual Review of United Nations Affairs*, 62.

111. O. Obasanjo, *Address to the U.N. General Assembly*, 32nd Session (New York, October 13, 1977) 4.

112. *Federal Ministry of Information News Release No. 1887*, 21 October 1977, 4.

113. Aminu Tiijani and D. Williams Shehu Shagari: My vision of Nigeria, ed. (London: Frank Cass, 1981) 59.

114. Aminu Tiijjani and D. Williams *Shehu Shagari: My vision of Nigeria*, 56.

115. Secretary General, Kurt Waldheim told the Security Council on November 24, 1980 that South Africa and SWAPO had agreed to attend the proposed U.N.—sponsored conference in January.

116. "Namibia Conference Ends after Failing to Agree on Central Issues," *United Nations Chronicle* XVIII, 3 (N) (March 1981): 5.

117. "Namibia Conference Ends after Failing to Agree on Central Issues."

118. "Namibia Conference Ends after Failing to Agree on Central Issues."

119. "Assembly, In Resumed Session, Calls for Total Sanctions Against South Africa," *United Nations Chronicle XVIII*, 5(N) (May 1981): 5–7.

120. "Waiting for Reagan," *The Economist*, 22 November 1980, 41–42.

121. Ali A. Mazrui, "Africa between Republican and Democratic Administrations," *Africa Report* (January–February 1981): 46.

122. Richard Deutsch, "Reagan and Africa," *Africa Report* (January-February 1981): 4–6.

123. "U.S. Uses 'Constructive Engagement' Policy with South Africa," *Africa Report* (July–August 1981): 23.

124. "Africa: The Namibian Conundrum," *Newsweek*, 15 November 1982, 71–74.

125. Assistant Secretary, Chester Crocker, "U.S. Interests in Africa," *Council on Foreign Relations*, New York (Current Policy No. 330), 5 October 1981, 3.

126. Assistant Secretary, Chester Crocker, "U.S. Interests in Africa., 7.

127. The Brazzaville Protocol.

128. Roger Murray, "No easy Path to Independence," *Africa Digest* (May–June 1977): 19 and cited by Allan Cooper in "U.S. Economic Power and Political Influence in Namibia" (Ph. D. dissertation, Atlanta University 1981) 145.

129. Allan Cooper, "U.S. Economic Power and political Influence in Namibia" (Ph. D. dissertation, Atlanta University 1981), 147.

130. Barbara Rogers, *Foreign Investment in Namibia* (New York: U.N. Council for Namibia, 1975), 10 and cited by Allan Cooper, 149.

131. Siedman, *Multinational Corporations*, 165.

132. Cooper, "U.S. Economic Power," 164.

133. Cornelius W. Dekiewiet, *A History of South Africa* (New York: Preager, 1967, 4.

134. Tom Hopkinson, *South Africa* (New York: Time, Inc., 1964), 25.

135. Van den Berghe, *South Africa: A Study in Conflict* (Los Angeles: UCLA Press, 1965) 14.

136. Leo Marquard, *A Short History of South Africa* (New York: Praeger, 1968), 15.

137. Leo Marquard, *A Short History of South Africa*, 15.

138. Gwendolen Carter, "South Africa: Growing Black-White Confrontation," *Southern Africa: The Continuing Crisis*, Gwendolen Carter and Patrick O' Meara, ed. (Bloomington: Indiana University Press, 1979), 98.

139. Senator Dick Clark (D., Iowa), Chairman of the Senate Foreign Relations Sub-Committee on African Affairs.

140. B. Magubane, *The Political Economy of Race and Class in South Africa* (New York: Monthly Review Press, 1979) 2.

141. T. Beard, "General Introduction," in *African Perspectives on South Africa*, Hendrik van der Merwe, ed. (London: Rex Collings, 1978) 8.

142. *The Report of the Study Commission on U.S. Policy Toward Southern Africa* (Los Angeles: UCLA Press, 1981) 49.

143. *The Study Commission on U.S. Policy Toward Southern Africa*, 49.

144. *The Study Commission on U.S. Policy Toward Southern Africa*, 50.

145. Berghe, *South Africa*, 133.

146. Magubane, *The Political Economy of Race and Class*, XII.

147. *The Study Commission on U.S. Policy toward Southern Africa*, 113.

148. "South Africa: Can Race War be avoided?" *Great Decisions 1981*, 35.

149. *Great Decisions 1981*, 35.

150. *The Study Commission on U.S. Policy Toward Southern Africa*, 197.

151. "Nigeria sends relief Aid to Nationalists," *New Nigerian*, September 10, 1977, 9.

152. *Times International*, 17 January 1977, 4.

153. *Report of the World Conference for Action Against Apartheid*, vol. 1 (New York: United Nations, 1977).

154. *West Africa* , 29 August 1977, 1791.

155. *Report of the World Conference for Action Against Apartheid*, vol. 11 (New York: United Nations, 1977) 13.

156. For details see *Report of the Conference*, vol.1 p. 31 Delegates from the West expressed reservations on some of the points and attempted to prevent total approval of the Lagos Declaration, which was eventually approved by acclamation.

157. "A Precise Move Against Barclays," *West Africa*, 3 April 1978, 636.

158. *New York Times*, 4 October 1980, 4 (A).

159. *The Study Commission on U.S. Policy Toward Southern Africa*, 144.

160. This was contained in an Amendment to the Bill of Authorization introduced by Representative Paul Tsonas (D. Massachusetts) in 1978. It had the support of national labor organizations, church groups and main-stream-to-liberal political forces.

161. The Rev. Leon H. Sullivan is the author of six principles promulgated in 1977 that form a code of conduct for American companies doing business in South Africa.

162. Secretary of State, Cyrus Vance, *U.S. Relations with Africa*, Address before the 58th annual meeting of the U.S. Jaycees in Atlantic City, 20 June 1978, 5.

163. "South Africa: Can Race War be avoided?" *Great Decisions* 1981, 40.

164. Henry Jackson, "Reagan's Policy Rupture," *Africa Report* (September–October 1981): 11.

165. Henry Jackson, "Reagan's Policy Rupture.

166. Hennie Serfontein, "Too Little Changes Too Late," *Africa*, 113 (N) (January 1981): 37.

167. Hennie Serfontein, "Too Little Changes Too Late."

168. Magubane, *The Political Economy of Race and Class*, 324.

169. Magubane, *The Political Economy of Race and Class*, 324.

170. *Africa Confidential*, 11 March 1981, 2.

171. Randall Robinson, "South Africa Under Botha: Investments in Tokenism," *Foreign Policy* (Spring 1980): 167.

172. James E. Baker et al., "The American Consensus on South Africa," *World View* (October 1979): 12.

173. CODESA participants included the South African government the African National Congress, the National Party, the South African Communist Party, the lukatha Freedom Party, and other minority parties.

174. The election was regarded as free and fair, but many of the thorny problems created by apartheid remained largely unresolved.

175. National Strategy Information Center, *The Resource War and the U.S. Business Community* (New York: 1980),14.

176. Cited by Seidman, *Multinational Corporations*, 76.

177. *The Study Commission on U.S. Policy Toward Southern Africa*, 394.

Chapter Five

Conclusion

In the course of pursuing its stated foreign policy objectives, Nigeria realized that there were other important actors in the international environment to contend with. One such actor was the United States. Nigeria's commitment to the cause of African emancipation seemed to have been in harmony with United States global policy which sought to: (a) foster closer cooperation with Nigeria, regarded as one of the influential states, able to sway the fate of the rest of Africa; and (b) enhance United States' cooperative effort with "moderate states of Africa in the cause of African emancipation."[1]

This convergence of interests formed the basis of Nigeria-United States relations during the period covered by this study. During this period both countries publicly took similar positions on the issue of political change in Africa. However, United States had some ulterior motives in taking these positions. Paramount were its profitable economic interests and strategic interests in the region. Sometimes genuine human rights concern were also motivating factors. On occasions, both countries made joint efforts to find peaceful solutions to the problem of political change in Africa.

How did these shared perspectives and the cooperative efforts between both countries impact the struggles in Angola, Zimbabwe, Namibia and South Africa? In this concluding chapter, an attempt will be made to: (a) summarize the roles played by Nigeria and the United States in the liberation struggles of these countries; (b) generalize about the relations between both countries with regard to political change in Africa, with an update on relations between the two countries after decolonization and, (c) critically evaluate the prospects for Nigeria-United States relations in the future.

ROLES PLAYED BY NIGERIA AND THE UNITED STATES

Angola

The Angolan crisis drove home the fact that "very rarely, if ever, is there either a total harmony or total conflict of national interests" between nations.[2] Nigeria and the United States initially backed the same faction (UNITA-FNLA), but for different reasons.

Nigeria: Earlier on in the struggle UNITA-FNLA was thought to have the best prospect of winning the elections. Furthermore UNITA had the largest popular support in Angola. United States: Concerns about Russian and Cuban involvement, and a feverish attempt to deny anti-western powers a strong foothold in Southern Africa; and varied economic and strategic interests in the region were important factors. However, South Africa's intervention in the Angolan crisis changed all that. Nigeria and the United States found themselves on the opposite sides of the conflict, with Nigeria backing the MPLA while the United States backed the UNITA-FNLA faction.

Perhaps more important was the fact that the Angolan crisis marked the beginning of a shift in United States' perspective on political change in Africa. Contrary to the Nixon administration's policy as outlined in NSSM 39 which predicted, inter alia, continued Portuguese domination, and ruled out black victory, United States not only witnessed the dismantling of Portuguese domination and the celebration of black victory, but it actively supported one of the factions vying for political power rather than attempting to prevent political change. Caught unawares by events in Angola, United States sought to install in Angola a neo-colonial government by covertly funding and arming FNLA-UNITA, the faction considered by the United States as a "moderate and pro-western in orientation." This led to a serious disagreement between Nigeria and the United States. This disagreement was important in that it clearly demonstrated that Nigeria was truly committed to real independence in Angola while the United States was prepared to settle for a neo-colonial pattern of political change.

There was a perception in the United States that an MPLA government in Angola would be inimical to United States' interests, but history proved that wrong. Thus, by backing the FNLA-UNITA United States sought to prevent the MPLA from coming to power or as John Stockwell, the former chief of the C.I.A.'s Angola Task Force, puts it, "to prevent the quick and cheap installation in Angola of what Mobutu would regard as a pawn of Moscow."[3] African interests and concerns were not the factors behind U.S. involvement in Angola.

United States anti-MPLA posture notwithstanding, the most important thing to the Angolan people and Pan-Africanists was true independence; how it occurred was of secondary significance. Historically, Pan-Africanists seemed to favor this stand, and Angola was not an exception. In Julius K. Nyerere's own words, "anything else, at this stage, is irrelevant to us." The concern, Nyerere asserted, was political change, not how it was won. After all, Nyerere added, "in the war against Nazism the United States and the 'Soviet Union' were allies."[4]

Events since Angola's independence in 1975 have been fairly consistent with this thinking, as has been the case with most African states that won the fight for political change through the assistance of Russia and Cuba. They invariably turned once again to the West for their technology, trading opportunities and economic assistance. Revolutionary rhetoric was toned down for political and economic reality because, in essence, "Africa is part of the non-communist world economic system."[5] According to United States Under Secretary for Political Affairs in the Carter administration,. Newsom, " a few African governments describe their policies or ruling parties as Marxist-Leninist or scientific socialist, but their policies are mixed and do not follow any rigid Saviet model."[6] These countries include Mozambique, Ethiopia and Angola. In these countries there was evidence "of resistance on the part of the leadership to the total adoption of the Marxist-Leninist pattern of internal policies and organization."[7] Andrew Young has long urged United States policymakers not to consider the socialist rhetoric of some African leaders in isolation, but rather to compare it with their actual policies. In 1976 Angola's President, Agostino Neto, defended Angola's independence and sovereignty when he pointed out that:

> We are free and independent. . . . We are not satellites because the 'Soviet Union' provides us with arms. We have never asked Moscow how we should organize our state. It is our movement, our government and our people who will take decisions on the many major problems which our country faces.[8]

Angolan overtures for direct discussions with the United States were conveyed through congressional aides and journalists touring Luanda. Soon after its independence in 1975 Angola expressed its: (a) readiness to welcome the Gulf Oil Corporation back to the Cabindan oil fields that it had left under United States government pressure; (b) recognition of the importance of Western markets for its oil, iron, coffee, diamond and other exports; and (c) willingness to make a constitutional undertaking not to allow any "foreign power to establish bases" on Angolan territory.[9] Gulf Oil Corporation came back to Angola and was pumping 160,000 barrels a day by 1981. Texaco and Boeing Aircraft also returned to do business in Angola.[10] Although these business interests do not speak for the United States, Gulf Oil Corporation's position on United States policy of nonrecognition was made known in 1978 when an official declared in congressional testimony that: "it would be in the mutual interest of the United States and Angola for the United States to establish formal relations with the People's Republic of Angola."[11]

However, while United States concern over Russian and Cuban involvement in Africa was understandable, this concern, as the study for the Defense Department by the Center for Strategic and International Studies pointed out, "should not be the only thrust of African policy. Furthermore, the study added, "not all activities of Moscow and Havana" in Africa "are counter to Untied States interests."[12] The crucial question was why had the United States not shown so much intensity and concern over the cause of Russian and Cuban involvement in Africa? It was clear that the existence of colonial and neo-colonial governments, occupation forces, settler regimes, and minority regimes presented the biggest opportunities for Russian and Cuban involvement in Africa. Emphasizing this point further, a study for the Defense Department declared that "the existence of white, minority-ruled governments is the cause of Russian and Cuban involvement, and as long as such governments exist and follow discriminatory policies" Africa will seek help from the Soviets and Cubans for their liberation.[13] In a belated attempt to remove the cause of Soviet and Cuban involvement in Africa United States steadily increased its role in finding a peaceful solution to African problems after the Angolan crisis.

On the whole, Nigeria-United States role in Angola had different impacts on the resolution of the conflict. U.S. continued support for FNLA-UNITA, long after the MPLA had won the war and, this had the negative impact of prolonging the war and destabilizing the MPLA government. Nigeria's strong position in favor of the winning faction, (MPLA) whose objectives were true independence and self-determination had the positive impact of helping fellow Africans to liberate themselves from colonialism and oppression.

However, in the case of Zimbabwe, Nigeria-United States differences were not as sharp as they were in Angola. Thus, both countries made joint efforts to find a peaceful solution to the crisis.

Zimbabwe

When President Carter came into office in 1977 he explained to an understandably skeptical Africa that the motivating force in United States policy in Africa was not opposition to communism per se, but concern for the aspirations of the continent. Andrew Young's appointment and his subsequent diplomacy were instrumental in lending credibility to this new United States line. And when the situation in Zimbabwe became critical in 1977, Nigeria and the United States had no major difficulty in making a joint effort to find a peaceful solution to the problem.

First, there was the basic agreement between both countries that: (a) political change in Zimbabwe was inevitable; and (b) such change should be fundamental. Second, both countries were also agreed that the solution that would bring about such a change should be one which was acceptable to all parties to the conflict, and to devise such a peace plan, all the parties to the conflict, would be brought to the conference table.

It was under this basic understanding and commitment to meaningful change by both countries that their collaborative efforts to find a peaceful solution to the Zimbabwean problem, as demonstrated by the many diplomatic initiatives including the Anglo-American Proposals and the Lancaster House Agreement, were successful. The outcome in Zimbabwe, for which Nigeria and the United States were given a substantial part of the credit, was a desirable one. First, it settled once and for all, the issue of political change in Zimbabwe, thereby meeting the aspirations of the Zimbabwean people, the foreign policy objective of Nigeria and at the same time enhanced the credibility of United States global policy in the region. Second, in the words of Andrew Young, it "was the premier achievement in the long struggle for majority rule in Southern Africa, and United States role in that process contributed to the success" in Zimbabwe.[14] Furthermore, the success of United States diplomatic initiative in Zimbabwe, according to Xan Smiley, entailed considerable political benefits for the West, in that: "Mugabe has, in fact, been cold toward the 'U.S.S.R.' since independence. His refusal to invite delegations from the "Soviet Union's" closest Eastern bloc allies to independence celebrations was widely seen as a snub."[15] The thinking in the State Department was that: . . . our security has been enhanced by the success of peacemaking in Zimbabwe. The effort deprived our adversaries of a conflict to exploit . . . we must not retreat from those efforts.[16]

As in Angola, events since independence in Zimbabwe have shown that revolutionary rhetoric during the struggle for political change does not necessarily translate into Marxist-Leninist policies patterned after the Russian model. Rather, President Mugabe "has spoken of his high esteem for the Untied States and his desire to form genuine bonds of friendship with America." Furthermore, he made known "his intention to work within the free enterprise system."[17] The United States responded with a total of $20 million in assistance in 1979 and $30 million in 1980.[18] Nigeria also gave assistance to Zimbabwe, including a $5 million grant "to enable the government to buy out the South African stake in Zimbabwe's newspapers" in 1980.[19]

It was unlikely that the outcome in Zimbabwe would have been the same without the efforts of the Patriotic Front, the Front Line States, Nigeria and the United States. Independence in Zimbabwe, as Andrew Young puts it, was a victory for diplomacy, but it was also a victory for armed struggle, in that:

> . . . it was achieved through the skilled and tough diplomacy of the British government . . . the patient statesmanship of the Front Line states and Nigeria; the courage and unshakable commitment to liberation shown by Rovert Mugabe (PF) . . . and the firm, consistent support of the United States government.[20]

With the exception of South Africa, where the mood was decidedly one of somber caution, reactions elsewhere in Africa were very enthusiastic.[21] African Union saw the outcome in Zimbabwe as a vindication of its position that the Patriotic Front was the "sole and legitimate representative of the Zimbabwean people."[22] In his congratulatory message, Lesotho's chief Leabua Jonathan saw the outcome in Zimbabwe as "a victory for all black people in Southern Africa and definite defeat for the forces of racism."[23] Anwar Sadat of Egypt called the outcome in Zimbabwe "the culmination of an honest struggle by the people of Zimbabwe under the leadership of the Patriotic Front."[24] Colin Legum, who had concluded in the previous year (1979) that "the chances of a negotiated settlement in Rhodesia" would take a miracle, called the outcome in Zimbabwe an astonishing achievement" and gave credit to Britain, the Commonwealth, the Front Line states, Nigeria, the United States and the Patriotic Front. Specifically, Legum pointed out two critical factors:

> . . . the confluence of interests which in the past had been strongly divergent; and the co-incidence of a number of leaders holding their particular positions at the point where the armed struggle of the Patriotic Front(PF) had succeeded in weakening the capacity of the defending Rhodesian forces to hold out much longer.[25]

The impact of the collaborative efforts of Nigeria and the United States on the Zimbabwean situation can be said to have been constructive and instrumental. These efforts, according to O. Aluko, "were among the decisive ones."[26] Because of these efforts, echoed the *New York Times*, "Rhodesia has been reborn as Zimbabwe. Most important, it has been born free."[27]

Furthermore, the outcome in Zimbabwe was very gratifying to nationalists and prominent blacks in the region who considered it as a giant psychological boost for black aspirations in Namibia and South Africa itself, and hoped that the South African government would draw the appropriate lesson from it."[28] Dr. N. Motlana of Soweto said "I am as happy as anybody could ever be—as happy as when Frelimo won in Mozambique." An important lesson South Africa should have learned from the outcome in Zimbabwe, according to Motlana, "is that the black puppets whom whites imposed on blacks as their leaders could not work." He also expressed the hope that the outcome in Zimbabwe would make "South African blacks realize that they would also be victorious one day."[29] The Star perhaps summed up the prevailing feelings among black people in South Africa when it editorialized that:

> The first lesson from this is that South African government must negotiate directly and immediately with the real black leaders in this country, not just those traditional leaders and obvious moderated through whom the National Party hopes to achieve some vaguely defined ethnic 'constellation' of states.[30]

As it turned out, South Africa did not, of its own volition, negotiate "directly and immediately with the real black leaders" of South Africa. An escalation of domestic violence and an increase in external pressure on the South African regime brought this about.

Namibia

In Namibia, United States was an active member of the Contact Group; and a major force in the drafting of the Group's proposal for a Namibian settlement. Donald McHenry's role in this group was instrumental to the success of United States diplomatic initiative. He was credited with: (a) convincing South Africa and SWAPO to agree to the Group's peace proposal; (b) persuaded South Africa "that a United Nations-approved and supervised" peace plan would be in the best interest of South Africa; and (c) brought the two parties to the conflict "within sight of the peace table, and kept them there through two and half years of complex and bitter negotiations."[31] Nigeria-United States collaborative efforts, with cooperation from the Untied Nations produced some degree of success. First, South Africa was moved grudgingly from outright intransigence to doubtful cooperation, and participated in all party conference in 1981. Second, South Africa was forced to come to grips about the inevitability of Namibia's independence.

None of these would have been thinkable without U.S. pressure and the international community's diplomatic efforts in which Nigeria and the Untied States were a major force. But these effects seemed to have dissipated with Reagan in the White House. He made Namibian independence a non-priority issue and relaxed pressure on the South African government. In effect, Reagan rolled back what little progress had been made towards Namibia's independence during the previous administration. Even Reagan's "constructive engagement "and linkage formula could not stop the Namibian freedom train. Perhaps the point where Nigeria-United States shared perspective and cooperative efforts needed to make a stronger impact than it actually did was South Africa itself.

South Africa

The manifestations of this impact can be gleaned from Prime Minister P.W. Botha's now famous "adapt or die" speech, in which he indicated that he clearly understood the need for far-reaching changes in the apartheid system. By early 1980 South Africa's political fortunes appeared to be on the decline, with aspects of apartheid undergoing some changes. Piet Koornhof, the then South African minister for Cooperation and Development "declared war" on the pass system and petty apartheid. At the same time South Africa attempted to head off the increasingly militant and violent challenge of the ANC and its supporters. Observers likened the situation South Africa was confronted with in 1980 to that which de Tocqueville had described over a century ago when he wrote:

> Experience teaches us that, generally-speaking the most perilous moment for bad government is one when it seeks to mend its ways. Only consummate statecraft can enable a king to save his throne when, after a long spell of oppressive rule, he sets out to improve the lot of his subjects. Patiently endured so long as it seemed beyond redress, a grievance comes to appear intolerable once the possibility of removing it crosses men's minds.[32]

Perhaps the most striking indication that South Africa was entering this new era was found in its changed political perspective. Colin Legum summed up this change as follows: "whereas before there was a confident, even arrogant, assumption about the durability of white supremacy; now the dominant white group found itself on the defensive—no longer even sure of its own future."[33]

The success of liberation struggle in Southern Africa also had its impact, particularly on the perceptions of South African blacks. T. Beard explained this changed perceptions accurately when he wrote: For the first time for well over a decade, blacks have begun to question the immutability of white domination and to anticipate processes of change in which their roles will not be those of mere subordinates dictated to by a 'white' government.[34]

Consequently, there was a growing acceptance of revolutionary violence among blacks. They believed that fundamental change would be brought about through revolutionary means. *The Report of the Study Commission on United States Policy toward Southern Africa* explained that:

> . . . among young urban blacks, the watchword that has been gaining currency is 'which side of the gun are you on?' Africans began leaving South Africa for military training abroad about 1973 . . . during the two years after Soweto. . . . Some 4,000 Africans left the Witwatersrand for such training.[35]

This changed perceptions, coupled with the rise in expectations among blacks in South Africa, which found expression through heightened violence, remained unbroken by government counter-measures. It was true in 1949 when Kwame Nkrumah made the point as it was in 1981:

> When a people who have smarted under a foreign rule suddenly wake up to the indignities of such a rule and begin to assert their national and inherent right to be free then they have reached that stage of their political development when no amount of oppressive laws and intimidation can keep them down. . . . When the spirit of the oppressed people revolts against its oppressors that revolt continues until freedom is achieved. It carries in its wake a force too dangerous to suppress.[36]

It was under these circumstances that South Africa sued for peace, culminating in the election of 1994. The combined effect of the successes of the liberation fighters and international pressure precipitated the outcome in South Africa.

A GENERALIZATION

On balance, Nigeria-United States relations with respect to political change in Africa were marked by disagreements and cooperation. Specifically, relations were decidedly cool at times, as during the Nixon-Ford era; cordial at other times, as they were during the Carter administration, and conflictual during the Reagan and Bush administrations.

For different reasons, the two nations shared, as President Carter puts it: "(a) a commitment to majority rule and individual human right, (b) a commitment to an Africa that is at peace, free from colonialism, and free from racism."[37] These commitments underlined their shared perspectives on political change in Africa. During the period under study both countries essentially worked closely together to achieve these goals in some of the cases studied and in other African troubled spots. They took similar positions on most of the cases, although there was a serious question mark over Untied States' motives; had serious disagreement over Angola, with the United States backing the faction with a neo-colonial orientation; fully collaborated in working out the peace plan in Zimbabwe and made some progress in Namibia and South Africa. President Carter reiterated that, "the United States remain committed, as do the people of Nigeria to the path of genuine progress and fairness" in Africa.[38] Although there were disagreements along the way, both countries' commitment to the cause of Africa emancipation paid off with the end of colonial era in Africa in 1990 and the last vestiges of white minority rule dismantled in 1994.

AFTER DECOLONIALIZATION: AN UPDATE

Although the parameters of this research centered on the years of decolonization in Africa that ended in 1994, it is perhaps in order to give a sketchy update of the relations between the two countries since then. With the end of the Cold War, the context of U.S. foreign policy shifted from cold war considerations to more idealistic notions of democratic governance, human rights and the rule of law.

Paradigm Shift: Democratic Governance and Human Rights

One of the primary interests of the United States is to have a stable, democratic government in Nigeria. This objective is premised on the assumption that political instability, if unchecked, could lead to the collapse of the Nigerian state. The corollary to that is a failed Nigerian state could have catastrophic consequences for U.S. interests in Africa. There was a lull in Nigeria-United States relations after minority rule was dismantled in South Africa. The Abacha junta squandered the goodwill that existed between the two countries with astonishing record of human rights abuses and the seemingly endless and meaningless transitions to democratic rule. Extrajudicial killings and arbitrary arrests were common. Many pro democracy and human rights activists and labor leaders were jailed. Relations between the two countries hit a new low when the presidential election of 1993 was annulled by Babangida. The execution of the Ogoni Nine including Ken Saro-Wiwa on November 10, 1995 was the final straw that put the relationship on ice. At first, U.S. strategy was "to do all that we can to persuade General Abacha to move toward general democracy and respect for human rights, release of political prisoners, and holding of elections."[39] When persuasion failed the Clinton administration opted for imposition of limited sanctions.

Limited Sanctions

The Clinton administration condemned the actions of the Nigerian military government and proposed limited diplomatic and economic sanctions, which included a cut off of Nigeria's access to World Bank and IMF loans, suspension of all economic, military assistance and travel restriction on all top government and military personnels. Critics charged that these actions did not go far enough. They called for oil embargo and a stop to new oil-related investments in Nigeria.[40] Several legislations were introduced in both Houses of Congress to tighten sanctions on Nigeria, but none made it to law. Two of the bills that were representative of the several bills introduced deserve some attention. The

House Bill, introduced by Rep. Donald Paine (D. New Jersey) and the Senate Bill introduced by Nancy Kassebauru (Rep. Kansas) were essentially identical, and if passed, would have simply turned the existing sanctions in place into law. The Clinton administration stock to its policy of constructive dialogue, and calls for oil embargo, freezing of Nigeria's assets in the U.S. largely went unheeded. However the administration made it clear to the Abacha junta that the endless transition program was unacceptable, particularly when it appeared Abacha was maneuvering to succeed himself as president. Dr. Susan Rice, Assistant Secretary of State for African Affairs in the Clinton administration, demanded that Abacha "undertake a genuine transition to civilian rule," and to "establish a level playing field by allowing free political activity, providing for an open press, and ending political detention"[41] Abacha died in June 1998 and was replaced by Abdulsalam Abubakar.

Improved Relations

With the death of Abacha, there was renewed optimism that Nigeria had a historic opportunity to succeed in its never ending search for democratic rule. Before Abubakar could fully explain his transition program, the U.S. restated its position that included three points, "freeing political prisoners, second, ensuring respect for the basic freedoms of speech, press and assembly, and third, returning the Nigerian army to its rightful position as a professional armed force committed to defending the constitution and civilian rule."[42] Abubakar was receptive to U.S. demands, and opened up the political process, released political prisoners and set the dates for elections.

In February 1999 Obasanjo was elected president by winning 62.8% of the votes, and was sworn in on May 29, 1999. Sanctions were lifted and closer ties between the two countries were reestablished. Echoing this new beginning, President Clinton said during a state visit to Nigeria on August 26, 2000: "We are rebuilding ties severed during years of dictatorship." America, he said:

> "know that after so many years of despair and plunder your journey has not been easy, but we are also committed to working with the people of Nigeria to help build stronger institutions, improve education, fight disease, crime and corruption, ease the burden of debt and promote trade and investment in a way that brings more of the benefits of prosperity to people who have embraced democracy."[43]

Areas of Interest

United States current policy toward Nigeria is centered on multiple and diverse interests: (1) promotion of democratic governance and human rights

(2) economic interests. (3) curbing narcotics trafficking and financial crimes (4) support for U.S. diplomatic initiatives in the region, including peace keeping operations and (5) support for U.S. counter terrorism policy. Nigeria has cooperated with the U.S. in many important U.S. diplomatic initiatives in its role as a regional power, played pivotal role in peacekeeping operations in Africa; sending troops to regional trouble spots in Chad, Liberia and Sierra Leone, and facilitated negotiations between the government of Sudan and the Darfur freedom fighters. Nigeria has spent over $10 billion and sacrificed hundreds of its soldiers' lives for peacekeeping operations in African trouble spots. Furthermore, Nigeria has given strong diplomatic support for U.S. counter-terrorism efforts, playing a leading role in West Africa. Its security forces collaborate with the U.S. by sharing intelligence on counter-terrorism issues, and are "proactive in investigating potential threats to U.S. interests." Nigeria condemned the terrorist attacks, and supported U.S. military action against the Taliban and Al- Quada, with the inherent political risk of alienating a segment of the Muslim population in the country. Nigeria has played a leading role in forging anti-terrorism consensus among the West Africa states.[44] Nigeria has cooperated with the United States in its campaign against international drug trafficking, having signed a mutual law enforcement agreement and a special anti-drug Memorandum of Understanding with the United States. United States efforts to fight financial crimes have also received assistance from the Nigerian government.

Convergence of Interests

There are points at which the two countries' interests converge. Two of such critical areas warrant our attention. First, the sale and purchase of Nigerian oil, second, the promotion and maintenance of democratic governance and human rights in Nigeria. Nigeria has enormous oil reserves, estimated at 40 billion barrels and produces about 2.4 barrels per day. And as of March 2007, Nigeria is the third largest supplier of oil to the United States, surpassing Venezuela and Saudi Arabia. The U.S. is Nigeria's largest customer, buying 40 percent of Nigeria's oil. Exxon Mobile and Chevron are the two major U.S. companies doing business in Nigeria, and U.S. total investments in oil related ventures in Nigeria is $7 billion.[45]

To protect U.S. investments, and for Nigeria to harness its enormous resources, distribute it equitably and deliver the peace and prosperity Nigerians have been yearning for would require a strong commitment by both countries to democratic governance, human rights, the rule of law, a free press, transparency and credible leadership.

While there is some convergence of interests between the two countries, Nigeria has specific interests such as support for debt relief or cancellation, poverty alleviation and trade and investments in the non-oil sector. Nigeria faces enormous economic challenges. Nigeria is almost at the bottom of all statistical indicators. The 2006 United Nations Human Development Report rank Nigeria 159 out of 177 nations. In 2005 Nigeria was ranked 158, meaning: "that for all practical purposes, the level of poverty, misery, and squalor in the population remained unchanged."[46] Nigerians living in poverty is about 70 percent. Schools and hospitals are ill-equipped, and infrastructures are in a bad state of repairs. Power and water supply are erratic. Nigeria earns $41.1 billion from oil and as much as 90 percent of that wealth is estimated to be in the foreign bank accounts of the corrupt elite who constitute about 10 percent of the population. Former dictator, Sani Abacha was reported to have stolen more than $3.5 billion. Nigeria has a depressingly long history of dictators who "have raped the nation and left it in a sordid state."[47] Nuhu Ribadu, Chairman of the Economic and Financial Crimes Commission (EFCC) said that, "Nigerian leaders have stolen about N65 trillion since Nigeria's independence in 1960."[48] Beyond swelling the foreign bank accounts of corrupt dictators, Nigeria's wealth also went into paying high interest on foreign loans, incurred by the dictators in the first place. However, in November 2005 Nigeria worked out a debt-relief deal with the Paris Club that eliminated $18 billion of its debts in exchange for $12 billion in payments. The total package was worth $30 billion out of Nigeria's total external debt of $37 billion.[49] In the end Nigeria spent a total of $5.1 billion on debt servicing before the loan was paid off on April 21, 2006.[50]

FUTURE PROSPECT

The chances of the close relations between Nigeria and the Untied States continuing in the future will largely depend on the achievement of both countries' objectives enumerated above. Of critical importance is the promotion and maintenance of democratic governance, economic development that would lead to equitable distribution of wealth, and protection of human rights in Nigeria. Everything else seems to hinge on Nigeria avoiding being a failed state. Nigeria's success or failure will have far reaching implications for the African continent. The U.S. can only pursue its varied diplomatic, economic and strategic interests in a stable, democratic and prosperous Nigeria. In a Congressional testimony in 1995, Assistant Secretary of State for African Affairs in the Clinton administration, George E. Moose said, "It is our firm belief that a democratic Nigeria that respects human rights and resolves issues of governance through the democratic process will create a context within which our other interests can be best pursued."[51] Already the CIA has predicted that Nigeria will break up, if current problems are not resolved. To sustain democratic governance in Nigeria, the U.S. must increase its economic assistance and continue to provide bilateral assistance in the training of elected officials in Nigeria on their roles and responsibilities in a representative democracy, assist in resolving the festering problem in the Niger Delta and reinforcing professionalism in the armed forces. United States economic assistance to Nigeria has not been substantial. Pakistan has received over $1 billion in economic assistance from the U.S. for its support for U.S. counterterrorism policy, but Nigeria has not been so generously rewarded for giving similar support. Nigeria needs U.S. support in tracking and returning stolen Nigerian funds in U.S. banks. Nigerian investigators have not received the full cooperation of U.S. law enforcement and treasury officials in this regard. United States policy on financial crimes should be reciprocal. Washington should provide the same level of assistance for Nigeria as it expects to receive from Nigeria on the war on financial crimes. Furthermore the U.S. should provide the same level of assistance to Nigeria that it provided the "Nazi Gold" investigation, returning all stolen funds and prosecute U.S. bank officials engaged in money laundering.

Although there is a decided paradigm shift in the context of Nigeria-United States relations after decolonization, with cold war considerations rendered untenable and replaced once again by idealism. However, motivations for U.S. policy in Nigeria have remained essentially the same: promotion of its varied economic, diplomatic and strategic interests. Clinton, like President Carter before him, injected a little idealism and a positive tone in U.S. policy toward Nigeria.

Nigeria and the United States have shared perspectives on political change in Africa during decolonization era, and both countries cooperated in the struggle for political freedom in Southern Africa. The United States supported prodemocracy groups during Nigeria's long struggle against military dictatorship, and also helped to put pressure on the military regimes in Nigeria to bring about reinstitution of democratic government. This relationship, built on shared interests, should be stronger and mutually beneficial, with both countries providing mutual support for each other' stated foreign policy objectives.

It is essential to have in the White House and Aso Rock administrations that would build on existing relationship to enthrone and strengthen democratic governance, economic development and human rights in Nigeria, create an enabling environment for majority of Nigerians to reap "democracy dividend," and for the United States to pursue its varied economic, diplomatic

and strategic interests. This policy should be grounded on genuinely recipro-
cal and mutually beneficial relationships, unaffected by the ideological ori-
entations of whoever is in the White House or Aso Rock.

NOTES

1. *National Security Memorandum No.* D. 18, 15.

2. Ivo Duchacek, *Nations and Men* (Hindsdale, Ill.: Dryden Press, 1975), 532.

3. Stockwell, *In Search of Enemies*, 54.

4. Julius K Nyerere, "American and Southern Africa," *Foreign Affairs* (July 1977: 35).

5. *Implications of Soviet and Cuban Activities in Africa for United States Policy*, A study for the Department of Defense by the Center for Strategic and International Studies, Washington, D.C., 1979, 25.

6. David D. Newsom, *Testimony before the Subcommittee on Africa of the House Committee on Foreign Affairs* on October 18, 1979, 5.

7. David D. Newsom, *Testimony before the Subcommittee on Africa of the House Committee on Foreign Affairs*.

8. "Angola Interview," *Africa Report* (January–February 1976): 3.

9. John Marcum, "Lessons of Angola," *Foreign Affairs* (April 1976): 420.

10. *New York Times*, 8 February 1981, Y. 25.

11. U.S. Congress, House Committee on International Relations, *U.S.-Angolan Relations*, Hearings before the Subcommittee on Africa, 95th Congress, 2nd Session, May 25, 1978, 39.

12. *Implications of Soviet and Cuban Activities*, 25.

13. *Implications of Soviet and Cuban Activities*, 25.

14. Andrew Young, "The U.S. and Africa: Victory for Diplomacy," *Foreign Affairs* (Winter 1981): 665.

15. Xan Smiley, "Zimbabwe, Southern Africa and the Rise of R. Mugabe," *Foreign Affairs* (Summer 1980): 1083.

16. Secretary of State, Ed. Muskie, "U.S. Security Programs," *Address Before the World Affairs Council*, Pittsburgh, 18 September 1980, 4.

17. *Department of State Bulletin*, June 1980, 19.

18. *Department of State Bulletin*, June 1980, 19.

19. Shehu Shagari, *My Vision of Nigeria*, 65.

20. Andrew Young, "U.S. and Africa," 650.

21. The O.A.U. and several African countries including Nigeria, Angola, and the Front Line States all sent messages of congratulations to Mugabe.

22. *The Daily News* (Tanzania), 4 March 1980, 3.

23. *The Guardian* (London), 5 March 1980, 5.

24. *Al Ahram* (Cairo, 4 March 1980, 2).

25. Colin Legum, *Africa Contemporary Records*:1979–1980 (New York: Africana Publishing Co., 1980), A3.

26. O.Aluko, "Britain, Nigeria and Zimbabwe," *African Affairs*, 1980, 91–102.

27. *New York Times*, 5 March 1980, 5Y.

28. Others able to express their views included Bishop Desmond Tutu, Gen. Secretary of the South African Council of Churches, who called on the South African government to welcome the new government in Zimbabwe with open and friendly arms.

29. *The Guardian*, 5 March 1980, 5.

30. *The Star*, 5 March 1980, 2.

31. Richard Deutsch, "High Stakes in Namibia," *Africa Report* (November–December 1979): 55.

32. Quoted in Economist, 21 June 1980, 3.

33. Colin Legum, "The Crisis of Afrikaner Survival," *Africa Contemporary Records* 1979–1980, .B.763.

34. Beard, "General Introduction," 2.

35. *The Report of the Study Commission on U.S. Policy Toward Southern Africa* (Los Angeles: UCLA Press, 1981), 199.

36. Kwame Nkrumah, *Revolutionary Path* (New York: International Publishers, 1973), 78.

37. President Jimmy Carter, "U.S. Commitment to Nigeria and Africa." *Public Papers of the Presidents*, (Washington, D.C.: The White House, 1980), 25.

38. President Jimmy Carter, "U.S. Commitment to Nigeria and Africa."

39. Ted Dagne, "Nigeria In Political Transitions," *CRS Issue Brief for Congress*, June 3, 2005, 12.

40. Cece M. Fadope, "Nigeria," *African Perspective*," Vol. 2, 12 (N), Jan. 1997, 3.

41. Ted Dagne, "Nigeria In Political Transitions," *CRS Issue Brief for Congress*, June 3, 2005, 12.

42. Ted Dagne, "Nigeria In Political Transitions."

43. President Clinton, Obasanjo Remarks in Abuja, Department of State, Aug. 26, 2000.

44. Jim Fisher-Thompson, Department of State, *Country Reports On Terrorism*, 2005.

45. Department of State, Bureau of African Affairs, "Background Note: Nigeria," September 2006, 5.

46. *The Guardian*, Editorial, "Improving the Quality of Life in Nigeria" Jan. 8, 2007.

47. *The Guardian*, "Improving the Quality."

48. *The Guardian*, "Improving the Quality."

49. CIA World Fact Book, Feb 8, 2007.

50. Daily Independent, Jan 26, 2006.

51. George E. Moose, Assistant Secretary State for African Affairs, "Assessment of U.S.-Nigeria Relations," *U.S. Department of State Dispatch*, July 31, 1995.

Bibliography

Ake, Claude. *Revolutionary Pressures in Africa*. London: Zed Press, 1978.

Allen, Christopher. *Radical Africana*. London: Merlin Press, 1974.

———. *Essays in Nigerian Foreign Policy*. Boston: Allen & Erwin, 1981.

Aluko, Olajide. "Britain, Nigeria and Zimbabwe." *Africa Affairs* (January 1980): 91.

Al Ahram, March 4, 1980, 2.

Atlanta Constitution, January 27, 1981, 4A; May 16, 1981, 6(A).

Africa, December 1975, March, July 1976, June 1978, July, November 1980, January and April 1981.

Africa Report, January–February 1976, November–December 1979, January–February 1980, July–August 1980, January–February 1981, July–August 1981.

Africa Confidential, October 1, 1980.

Africa Perspectives, vol. 2, 12 (N), Jan. 1977, 3.

Atlas World Press Review, July 1978.

Address to the Nation by Olusegun Obasanjo, "Federal Ministry of Information Release," No. 780, June 29, 1976.

Bailey, Thomas. *A Diplomatic History of the American People*. Englewood Cliffs: Prentice-Hall, 1974.

Bender, Gerald. *Angola Under the Portuguese*. Los Angeles: UCLA Press, 1978.

Berghe, Van den. *South Africa: A Study in Conflict*. Los Angeles: UCLA Press, 1965.

Brett, E.A. *Colonialism and Underdevelopment in East Africa*. London: Heinemann Press, 1973.

Boulding, Kenneth. *Conflict and Defense: A General Theory*. New York: Harper & Row, 1962.

Baker, James E.; de St. Jorre, John; and O'Flaherty, Daniel. "*The American Consensus on South Africa.*" *World View* (October 1979): 12.

Black Scholar, September 1978.

Carroll, Faye. *South West Africa and the United Nations*. Lexington: University of Kentucky Press, 1967.

CIA World Factbook, Feb. 8, 2007.

Cooper, Alan. *U.S. Economic Power and Political Influence in Namibia.* Ph. D. dissertation, Atlanta University, 1981.

Clington, Mario de Souza. *Angola Libre?* Paris: Gaillimard Press, 1975.

Cottam, Richard. *Foreign Policy Motivations: A General Theory and Case Study.* Pittsburgh: University of Pittsburgh Press, 1977.

Cervenka, Zdenek. *The Unfinished Quest for Unity: Africa and the OAU.* New York: Africana Press, 1977.

Crocker, Chester, and Lewis, W. "Missing Opportunities in Africa." *Foreign Policy* (Winter 1977–78): 142.

Congressional Quarterly, December 20, 27, 1975; January 31, 1976, May 19, 1979.

Constitution of the Federal Republic of Nigeria, Lagos: Federal Ministry of Information, Printing Division, 1979.

CRS Issue Brief for Congress, June 3, 2005, 12.

Davidson, Basil. *In the Eye of the Storm.* New York: Doubleday, 1972.

Davis, Gordon; Melunsky, L.; and du Randt, F.B. *Urban Native Law.* Port Elizabeth, South Africa: Grotius Publications, 1959.

DeKiewiet, Cornelius W. *A History of South Africa.* New York: Praeger, 1967.

Duchacek, Ivo. *Nations and Men.* Hindsdale, Ill.: Dryden Press, 1975.

Department of State Bulletin, August 1975; February 16, 1976; May 31, 1976; June 20, 1977 and July–August 1978, July 31, 1995, Aug. 26, 2000, Sept. 2006.

Daily News, March 4, 1980, 3.

Daily Telegraph, January 31, 1977; January 26, 1979, 5; June 14, 1979, 10.

Daily Independent, Jan. 26, 2006, 1.

Daily Times, September 8, 1977, 2; July 5, 1979, 2.

Economist, March 4, 18, 1978; May 26; July 7, 1979; November 22, 1980.

Ebinger, Charles. "External Intervention in Internal War: The Politics and Diplomacy of the Angolan Civil War." *Orbis* (Fall 1976): 671.

Fanon, Frantz. *The Wretched of the Earth.* New York: Grove Press, 1968.

Financial Mail, August 17, 1979, 2.

Good, Robert C. *U.D.I.: The International Politics of the Rhodesian Rebellion.* Princeton: Princeton University Press, 1973.

Guardian, August 22, 1978, 10; December 1, 1978, 5; March 5, 1980, 5.

Garba, Joseph. Address to the U.N. Security Council Meeting: On Mozambique's Complaint about Rhodesian Aggression, June 29, 1977.

Great Decisions: 1981.

Herald, February 14, 1979, 1.

Holsti, K.J. *International Politics: A Framework for Analysis.* Englewood Cliffs: Prentice-Hall, 1977.

Hopkinson, Tom. *South Africa.* New York: Time, Inc., 1964.

Hawley, Edward; Shepherd, George; and Mphahlele, E. "Angolan Independence: Agony and Hope." *Africa Today* (October 1975): 7.

Herskovits, Jean. "Nigeria: Africa's New Power." *Foreign Affairs* (January 1975): 314.
———, "Dateline Nigeria: A Black Power" *Foreign Policy* (Winter 1977–78) 167.

Implications of Soviet and Cuban Activities in Africa for U.S. Policy, Center for Strategic and International Studies, Washington, D.C., 1979.

International Herald Tribune, October 3, 1980, 4.

Jackson, Henry. *From the Congo to Soweto: U.S. Foreign Policy Toward Africa Since 1960*. New York: W. Morrow, 1982.

Johnson, William. "Namibia: Forces and Factions." *Africa Today* (August 1979): 23.

Kapungu, Leonard. *Rhodesia: The Struggle for Freedom*. New York: Orbis Books, 1979.

Kaplan, Irving. *Angola: A Country Study*. Washington, D. C.: American University Press, 1979.

Rhodesia: A Country Study. Washington D.C.: American University Press, 1979.

Kilson, Martin. *Political Change in a West African State*. Cambridge, Mass.: Harvard University Press, 1966.

Legum, Colin. *After Angola: The War over Southern Africa*. New York: Africana Publishers, 1976.

Lovell, John P. *Foreign Policy in Perspectives*. New York: Holt, Rinehart & Winston Press, 1970.

Los Angeles Times, December 17, 1978, part V. 2.

"Lusaka Manifesto on Southern Africa:" Joint Statement by the OAU Assembly of Heads of State and Government, Lusaka, Zambia, April 16, 1969.

Mugubane, Bernard. *The Political Economy of Race and Class in South Africa*. New York: Monthly Review Press, 1979.

Marcum, John. *The Angolan Revolution*. Vols. 1, 11. Cambridge, Mass.: MIT Press, 1978.

Marguard, Leo. *A Short History of South Africa*. New York: Praeger, 1968.

Merwe, van der Hendrick, ed. *African Perspectives on South Africa*. London: Rex Collings, 1978.

Martin, David, and Johnson, Phyllis. *The Struggle for Zimbabwe*. New York: Monthly Review Press, 1981.

Mason, Philip. *The Birth of a Dilemma*. New York: Praeger, 1958.

Morgenthau, Hans J. *Dilemmas of Politics*. Chicago: University of Chicago Press, 1958.

———. *Politics Among Nations*. New York: Alfred Knopf Press, 1973.

Mtshali, Vulindlela B. *Rhodesia: Background to Conflict*. New York: Hawthorn Books, 1967.

Marcum, John. "Lessons of Angola." *Foreign Affairs* (April 1976): 414.

Macebuh, Stanley. "Misreading Opportunities in Africa." *Foreign Policy* (Winter 1977–78): 162.

Myers, D., and Liff, D. "South Africa under Botha: The Press of Business." *Foreign Policy* (Spring 1980): 143.

Nelson, Harold. *Area Handbook for Southern Rhodesia*. Washington, D.C.: American University Press, 1975.

———, *Nigeria A Country Study*. Washington, D.C.: American University Press, 1982.

New Nigerian, February 4, 1977 ,1; September 10, 1977, 9; June 6, 1979 3.

New York Times, February 7, 1979, 10 (A); March 5, 1980.5(Y); October 4, 1980, 4(A), 1981,4 (Y).

Nigeria Standard, August 12, 1076, 5.

Nkrumah, Kwame. *Revolutionary Path*. New York: International Publishers, 1973.

Nyerere, Julius. "America and Southern Africa." *Foreign Affairs* (July 1977): 35.

"*National Security Council Strategy No. D. 18*," Washington, D.C., U.S. Government Printing Press, 1978.

National Security Council Inter-Department Group for Africa, "Study in Response to NSSM 39: Southern Africa," AF-NSE-1969, August 15, 1969.

"New Proposals for a Settlement: British Government White Paper," London, September 1977.

Nation, December 30, 1978.

New African, January 1982.

Newsweek, November 15, 1982.

The Nature and Extent of the South African Defense Forces' Involvement in the Angolan Conflict, "Defense Headquarters Communiqué," Pretoria, February 3, 1977.

Nigeria: Bulletin on Foreign Affairs, August–December, 1975; September 1977; January 1976.

Oyediran, Oyeleye, ed. *Nigerian Government and Politics*. London: Mcmillan Press, 1979.

Ohaegbulam, Festus. *Nigeria and the U.N. Mission to the Congo*. Tampa: University Press of Florida, 1982.

Obasanjo, Olushegun. Address to the Nation, Federal Ministry of Information Release, No. 780, June 29, 1976.

O'Meara, Patrick. *Rhodesia: Racial Conflict or Co-Existence?* New York: Cornell University Press, 1975.

Rand Daily Mail, May 16, 1980, 2.

Robinson, Randall. "South Africa under Botha: Investments in Tokenism." *Foreign Policy* (Spring 1980): 167.

Rotberg, Robert. "South Africa under Botha: How Deep a Change?" *Foreign Policy* (Spring 1980): 126.

Report of the OAU Conciliation Commission's Recommendations on Angola, Adopted at the OAU Summit in Kampala, October 24, 1975.

Report of the international Court of Justice on South West Africa, Second Phase, Judgment, 1966.

Report on the Native Problems in the Portuguese Colonies, Lisbon, 1970.

Report of the Study Commission on U.S. Policy Toward Southern Africa, Los Angeles: UCLA Press, 1981.

Report of the World Conference for Action against Apartheid, Vols. 1 and 11, New York: U.N. Press, 1977.

Report on The Rhodesian Election, Catholic Institute for International Relations, London, and April 1979.

Saul, John, and Gelb, Stephen. *The Crisis in South Africa: Class Defense, Class Revolution*. New York: Monthly Review Press, 1981.

Shagari, Shehu. Address presented by the president at the Commonwealth Heads of Government Conference in Melbourne, Australia, October 1981.

Siedman, Ann and Siedman, Neva. *South Africa and U.S. Multinational Corporations*. West Port, Conn.: Lawrence Hill & Co., 1978.

Schelling, Thomas. *Arms and Influence*. New Haven: Yale University Press, 1966.

Singer, David. *Deterrence, Arms Control and Disarmament*. New Haven: Yale University Press, 1970.

Stremlau, Hon. *The International Politics of the Nigerian Civil War*. Princeton: Princeton University Press, 1977.

——, *Survey of Nigerian Affairs*. Ibadon: Oxford University Press, 1978.

Smiley, Xan. "Zimbabwe, Southern Africa and the Rise of Robert Mugabe." *Foreign Affairs* (Summer 1980):1083.

Times, August 21, 1978, 9.

Times International, August 2, 1976, 3.

Thompson, Leonard, and Butler, Jeffery, eds. *Change in Contemporary South Africa*. Los Angeles: UCLA Press, 1975.

Time, April 30, 1979.

Tijjani, Aminu, and Williams, David, eds. *Shehu Shagari: My Vision of Nigeria*. London: Frank Cass, 1981.

Ufahamu, March 1971.

U.N. Chronicle, February 1976, December 1977, October 1978, March, May, and June 1981.

United Nations Resolution 1819 (XVII) "U.N. General Assembly Official Records," Vol. 1, 17th Session, 1962.

U.S. Congress, House. Testimony delivered by D.B. Easum before a "Hearing of the House of Representatives Sub-Committee on Africa," in Detroit, Michigan, April 29, 1981, U.S. Government Printing Office, Washington, D.C., 1981.

U.S. Congress, House. Testimony delivered by D. Newsom before the "Sub-Committee on Africa of the House Committee on Foreign Affairs," Washington, D.C., U.S. Government Printing Office, October 18, 1979.

U.S. Congress, House Committee on International Relations, "U.S. Angolan Relations," Hearing before the Sub-Committee on Africa, 95th Congress, 2nd Session, May 25, 1978.

U.S. Congress, Senate. Sub-Committee on African Affairs, "Imports of Minerals from Southern Africa by the U.S. and OECD Countries," September 1980.

U.S. President. "Public Papers of the Presidents of the U.S., Book 11, Washington D.C., U.S." Government Printing Office, 1979.

Vance, Cyrus "*The U.S. and Africa: Building Positive Relations*," Address at the Annual Convention of the NAACP, St. Louis, Mo., July 1, 1977.

Wayas, Joseph. *Nigeria's Leadership Role in Africa*. London: Mcmilllan Press, 1979.

Wheeler, Douglas, and Pelissier, R. *Angola*. New York: Praeger, 1971.

Washington Post, August 20, 1976, 7 (A); December 12, 1979, 5 (A).

World Today, January 1980, May and October 1980.

West Africa, August 29, 1977; April 3, 1978; August 6, 1979; July 27, November 2, 23, 1981.

Young, Andrew. "The U.S. and Africa: Victory for Diplomacy." *Foreign Affairs* (Winter 1981): 665.

Index

www.ingramcontent.com/pod-product-compliance
Lightning Source LLC
Chambersburg PA
CBHW021821270326
41932CB00007B/289